USE AI AS A TOOL TO HELP YOU NOT TO REPLACE YOU

COPYRIGHT PAGE

"Artificial Intelligence is not a replacement for human ingenuity—it is a mirror that reflects our wisdom, our flaws, and our potential. The challenge is not to fear AI, but to guide it with purpose."

INDEX

Introduction

- **Diving Deeper: Seeing AI as Our Empowering Partner**

    We're living in a time where technology is leaping forward at an astonishing pace, and at the heart of this transformation is artificial intelligence, or AI. It's not just a passing trend or a futuristic concept; AI is rapidly becoming a fundamental part of our lives, reshaping how we work, live, and interact with the world around us. Instead of viewing AI as a force that will replace human effort, we need to understand it as a powerful tool that can amplify our abilities, streamline our processes, and enhance our decision-making.

- **Understanding the Core of A**

    AI is a broad term that encompasses a wide range of technologies and methodologies designed to mimic human cognitive functions. It's about creating systems that can understand and generate human language, analyze vast datasets to predict future trends, and learn, reason, and act in ways that parallel human

2

intelligence. This multidisciplinary field draws on expertise from computer science, mathematics, psychology, neuroscience, and more, to build systems that can perform tasks once thought to be exclusively human.

The journey of AI began in the mid-20th century, with pioneers like John McCarthy coining the term 'artificial intelligence' at the landmark Dartmouth Workshop in 1956. This event marked the official birth of AI as a distinct field of study, sparking decades of relentless research and innovation. Over the years, AI has evolved from simple rule-based systems to sophisticated machine learning algorithms that can process immense amounts of data and make autonomous decisions.

- ## A Historical Look at AI's Evolution

The evolution of AI can be traced through several key milestones. In its early days, researchers focused on developing algorithms that could mimic human reasoning through logical deductions. However, these early systems often struggled with the complexity and scale of real-world problems. The 1980s saw a resurgence of interest in AI, particularly with the Japanese government's ambitious Fifth Generation Computer Systems Project, which aimed to create computers capable of human-like reasoning and language processing.

The advent of the World Wide Web in the 1990s revolutionized access to information, providing a fertile ground for AI development. The availability of vast datasets enabled researchers to explore new techniques, particularly in machine learning, which allows systems to learn from data rather than relying solely on pre-programmed rules. This paradigm shift laid the groundwork for the AI breakthroughs we witness today.

- ## The Vast Potential of AI: Transforming Lives and Industries

AI has the potential to revolutionize various aspects of our lives. In the realm of personal productivity, AI-powered virtual assistants can help us manage our schedules, automate mundane tasks, and provide instant access to information. In transportation, self-driving cars promise to enhance safety and efficiency, potentially reducing traffic accidents and congestion. In healthcare, AI-driven diagnostic systems can assist medical professionals in identifying diseases with greater accuracy, ultimately improving patient outcomes.

The applications of AI extend far beyond these examples. Industries such as finance, agriculture, education, and entertainment are leveraging AI to optimize operations, enhance customer experiences, and drive innovation. As AI continues to evolve, its integration into our daily lives will become increasingly seamless, fundamentally altering how we work, communicate, and interact with the world around us.

- ## Navigating the Challenges: Ethical and Practical Considerations

Despite its vast potential, the rise of AI is not without challenges. One of the most pressing issues is the development of systems that can genuinely understand and reason about the complexities of the world. While AI excels at pattern recognition and data analysis, it often struggles with tasks that require common sense reasoning or contextual understanding.

Ethical considerations also loom large in the discourse surrounding AI. As AI systems become more integrated into decision-making processes, concerns about bias, discrimination, and accountability arise. The algorithms that power AI can inadvertently perpetuate existing biases present in the data they are trained on, leading to unfair outcomes in areas such as hiring, law enforcement, and lending.

Moreover, the rapid advancement of AI raises questions about job displacement and the future of work. As machines become capable of performing tasks traditionally done by humans, there is a growing concern about the impact on employment and the need for workforce reskilling.

- ## A Collaborative Future: Humans and AI Working Together

The future of AI is characterized by uncertainty, yet it is clear that this technology will play a pivotal role in shaping our world. Rather than viewing AI as a threat to human employment, we must embrace it as a tool that can enhance our capabilities and improve our quality of life. By fostering a collaborative relationship between humans and AI, we can harness the strengths of both to create a more efficient, innovative, and equitable society.

To navigate the challenges posed by AI, it is essential to adopt a proactive approach. This includes developing AI systems that are transparent, fair, and accountable, as well as prioritizing ethical considerations in their design and deployment. Policymakers, technologists, and society at large must work together to establish guidelines and frameworks that ensure AI is used responsibly and for the benefit of all.

- Strategies for Empowering Ourselves with AI

As individuals and organizations embrace AI, it is vital to understand how to leverage this technology effectively. Here are several strategies for using AI as a tool for empowerment:

1. Education and Lifelong Learning: Continuous learning is essential in the age of AI. Individuals should seek to understand the fundamentals of AI, its capabilities, and its limitations. This knowledge will enable them to make informed decisions about how to integrate AI into their workflows and personal lives.
2. Collaborative Partnerships with AI: Rather than viewing AI as a competitor, individuals and businesses should see it as a collaborator. By utilizing AI to handle repetitive tasks, professionals can focus on higher-level strategic thinking, creativity, and interpersonal skills—areas where human intelligence excels.
3. Customization and Personalization: AI systems can be tailored to meet specific needs and preferences. By customizing AI tools, users can enhance their productivity and efficiency, ensuring that the technology aligns with their unique workflows and objectives.
4. Ethical Responsibility: As AI becomes more prevalent, it is crucial to prioritize ethical considerations in its application. Users should advocate for transparency in AI systems, ensuring that they are designed to be fair and unbiased. This includes being aware of the data used to train AI models and actively working to mitigate any biases present.
5. Embracing Adaptability: The landscape of work and society is evolving rapidly due to AI advancements. Individuals should cultivate a mindset that embraces change and adaptability, recognizing that the ability to learn new skills and adapt to new technologies will be key to remaining relevant in the workforce.
6. Community Engagement and Knowledge Sharing: Engaging with communities and networks focused on AI can provide valuable insights and support. By participating in discussions, attending workshops, and collaborating with others, individuals can stay informed about the latest developments and best practices in AI.
7. Leveraging AI for Social Good: AI has the potential to address some of the world's most pressing challenges, from climate change to healthcare disparities. Individuals and organizations should explore ways to use AI for social good, contributing to initiatives that promote sustainability, equity, and community well-being.

- ## The Dawn of New Possibilities

As we navigate the complexities of AI, it is essential to recognize its potential as a tool for empowerment rather than a replacement for human effort. By understanding AI's capabilities, embracing collaboration, and prioritizing ethical considerations, we can harness this technology to enhance our lives and create a better future. The journey ahead will require a collective effort to ensure that AI serves as a force for good, driving innovation and improving the human experience across the globe. Through proactive engagement and responsible use, we can shape a future where AI and humanity coexist harmoniously, unlocking new possibilities and opportunities for all.

I

The Amazing Journey

of AI

Introduction:-

The story of artificial intelligence, or AI, is like a really exciting adventure, full of smart ideas, big dreams, and a never-ending push to learn more. From its early days in the middle of the 20th century to being a game-changer in almost every part of our lives, AI has come a long way. In this section, we'll look at the important moments that shaped AI, the brilliant people and projects that made it happen, and the cool tech that led to the AI revolution we see today.

1.1 The Early Days of AI

1.1.1 Imagining Machines That Think

People have been curious about making machines that think like us for a very long time. Early thinkers wondered about how our minds work, which helped set the stage for AI. Philosophers like René Descartes thought about what makes us conscious, and mathematicians like Gottfried Wilhelm Leibniz imagined a way to use math to make machines think.

The idea of making smart machines really started to take off in the early 1900s, when we began to understand logic and how computers could work. People like George Boole, who invented Boolean algebra, and Alan Turing, who wrote a famous paper called 'Computing Machinery and Intelligence' in 1950, helped us see that machines could reason. Turing even came up with the Turing Test, which is a way to see if a machine can act so human that we can't tell it's not a person.

1.1.2 The Birth of Computer Science

The middle of the 20th century was a big deal because computer science became a real field of study. Building computers during World War II gave us the power we needed to start working on AI. Smart people like Alan Turing and John von Neumann came up with important ideas like algorithms, how computers work, and how to build them.

Turing's idea of a universal machine, which could do any kind of calculation, was super important. He designed the Turing Machine, which helped us understand how computers work and led to the creation of programming languages. Von Neumann's ideas about how to organize a computer's memory and processing parts became the standard for building computers, making it easier to create complex programs.

1.1.3 The First Steps in AI Research

In the beginning, AI researchers focused on creating programs that could think like humans. They wanted to make machines that could solve puzzles, play games, and figure things out logically. The first AI programs used rules and logic to make decisions, but they were limited by the computers of the time. They had trouble solving complicated problems, which made some researchers feel a bit discouraged.

One of the first AI programs was the Logic Theorist, made by Allen Newell and Herbert A. Simon in 1955. It was designed to prove math problems by thinking like a person. It actually proved 38 out of 52 theorems from a famous math book, showing that AI could handle tough logic problems.

1.2 The Dartmouth Workshop: Where AI Was Born

1.2.1 The 1956 Dartmouth Conference

A really important moment for AI happened in 1956, when John McCarthy, Marvin Minsky, Nathaniel Rochester, and Claude Shannon organized a workshop at Dartmouth College. This event is seen as the official start of AI as its own field of study. They brought together smart people to talk about how machines could think like humans.

The Dartmouth Conference had all kinds of people, including mathematicians, computer scientists, and brain researchers. They talked about how to make machines that could learn, think, and talk like us. They set big goals for AI, which shaped the future of AI research.

1.2.2 What is AI?

At the Dartmouth Conference, they came up with the name 'artificial intelligence' and set big goals for the field. They wanted to make machines that could think, learn, and talk like humans. This conference laid the groundwork for AI as a real field of study.

They thought AI could be achieved by using logic, neural networks, and clever ways to find solutions. They believed that by copying how humans think, machines could solve complex problems and do tasks that need intelligence. This idea of AI as a field with many different ways of doing things influenced AI research for many years.

1.2.3 The First AI Programs

After the Dartmouth Conference, researchers started making some of the first AI programs. Some important ones were:

- Logic Theorist (1955): Made by Allen Newell and Herbert A. Simon, this program proved math problems by thinking like a person. It proved 38 out of 52 theorems from a famous math book, showing that AI could handle tough logic problems.
- General Problem Solver (GPS) (1957) : Also made by Newell and Simon, this program tried to solve all kinds of problems. It used a method called means-ends analysis, showing that AI could be used in many different ways.

These early programs showed what AI could do, but also highlighted the limits of the technology at the time. Using only rules and logic made it hard for them to deal with things that were unclear and made it difficult for them to learn from experience.

1.3 The First AI Winter

1.3.1 Big Promises, Big Disappointments

Even though people were excited about AI at first, the field faced big challenges in the 1960s and 1970s. Researchers realized that the big goals they set at the Dartmouth Conference were hard to reach. The limitations of early AI programs became clear, leading to a period of disappointment called the 'first AI winter.'

During this time, it became obvious that real-world problems were very complex and the AI programs weren't good enough. AI programs couldn't learn from small amounts of data and needed a lot of human help, which made people doubt if we could ever make truly intelligent machines.

1.3.2 Less Money, Less Interest

As people saw the limits of AI, funding for research started to dry up. Governments and companies that had invested a lot of money in AI started to pull back. The lack of progress and the inability to deliver on promises led to less interest from researchers and the public.

This lack of funding forced many researchers to stop working on AI or switch to other areas of computer science. The excitement from the early days of AI was lost, and the field went through a period of slow progress.

1.3.3 The Impact of the First AI Winter

The first AI winter had a big impact on the field. Many researchers moved to other areas of computer science, and the early momentum was lost. However, some dedicated researchers kept exploring AI, laying the groundwork for future progress.

During this time, people started focusing on more practical uses of AI, like expert systems, which tried to capture human knowledge in specific areas. These systems used databases and reasoning engines to solve problems in fields like medicine and finance, showing that AI could still be useful despite the challenges.

1.4 The AI Comeback in the 1980s

1.4.1 The Japanese Fifth Generation Project

In the 1980s, AI made a comeback, mostly because governments started investing in it again. One of the biggest things that happened was the Japanese Fifth Generation Computer Systems (FGCS) project, which aimed to make computers that could reason and understand language like humans.

1.4.2 Big Goals

Started in 1982, the FGCS project was a big plan backed by the Japanese government, which spent about $850 million to develop advanced computer technology. The project's goals included making machines that could understand language, reason, and learn from experience. The FGCS wanted to make Japan a leader in computer technology and boost the economy through AI advancements.

The project aimed to create a new kind of computer that could process information like humans. Researchers wanted to make systems that could reason, learn, and communicate effectively, paving the way for more sophisticated AI.

1.4.3 New Tech Ideas

The FGCS project led to important advancements in areas like logic programming, knowledge representation, and expert systems. Researchers developed new programming languages, like Prolog, which made it easier to create AI programs that could reason and solve problems. The project also inspired research into knowledge-based systems, which tried to capture human expertise and make it accessible through AI.

The focus on representing knowledge and reasoning during this time helped build the foundation for more advanced AI. Researchers explored different ways to represent knowledge, which allowed for more flexible and dynamic reasoning.

1.4.4 Worldwide Impact

The FGCS project not only made AI exciting again in Japan but also had an impact around the world. It encouraged other countries, like the United States and European nations, to invest in AI research. This renewed interest led to the creation of AI research centers and projects worldwide, fostering teamwork and new ideas in the field. The competition from the FGCS project pushed researchers to explore new methods and applications, making AI research more vibrant and diverse.

1.5 The Rise of Machine Learning

1.5.1 Moving Away From Rule-Based Systems

As the 1980s went on, researchers realized that rule-based systems, which used rules and logic to make decisions, had limits. These systems had trouble adapting to new information and needed a lot of human help to update their knowledge. So, the focus shifted to machine learning, a part of AI that focuses on making programs that can learn from data.

Machine learning offered a more flexible way to do AI, allowing programs to get better over time as they saw more data. This was a big change from traditional AI, which often relied on fixed rules.

1.5.2 The Return of Neural Networks

The renewed interest in neural networks was a turning point in AI research. Inspired by how the human brain works, neural networks are made up of connected nodes that process information at the same time. Researchers started exploring different types of neural networks, which allowed for more complex pattern recognition and learning.

The development of multi-layer perceptrons (MLPs) and the use of activation functions allowed neural networks to model non-linear relationships in data. This opened up new possibilities for using AI in areas like image and speech recognition.

1.5.3 New Ways to Learn

The development of new ways to train neural networks, like backpropagation, made them much more effective. This allowed researchers to create models that could learn from large datasets, leading to big improvements in image and speech recognition. The ability to learn from data, instead of just using rules, opened up new possibilities for AI.

The use of techniques like dropout and L2 regularization also improved the performance of neural networks by preventing overfitting. These advancements made machine learning the most popular approach in AI research.

1.6 The Internet and the Data Explosion

1.6.1 The World Wide Web

The invention of the World Wide Web in the 1990s changed how we access information and data. The rapid growth of the internet provided a huge amount of knowledge, allowing researchers to collect and analyze large datasets. This data explosion was crucial for AI, because machine learning algorithms need a lot of data to learn.

The web made it easy to collect different kinds of data, like text, images, and videos, which became valuable resources for training AI models. The ability to access and process this data at scale transformed AI research and applications.

1.6.2 Big Data and AI

The idea of 'big data' came about as companies realized the value of the huge amounts of information generated online. Companies started collecting and analyzing data from various sources, like social media, online shopping, and sensors. This wealth of data provided a great opportunity for AI research, allowing for the development of more advanced models and applications.

Combining big data analysis with AI allowed companies to gain insights and make data-driven decisions. This combination has become a key part of modern business strategies, driving innovation and giving companies a competitive edge.

1.6.3 Data-Driven AI

As data became more available, AI research shifted to using data to drive progress. Researchers started developing algorithms that could automatically learn patterns and make predictions based on data. This shift laid the foundation for modern AI, where machine learning and deep learning are the main approaches.

Data-driven AI has led to big advancements in areas like natural language processing, computer vision, and recommendation systems. The ability to use large datasets for training has allowed AI systems to perform remarkably well in many different tasks.

1.7 The Deep Learning Revolution

1.7.1 Better Neural Networks

The 2010s saw a renewed interest in deep learning, a part of machine learning that focuses on training neural networks with many layers. These networks can learn complex patterns from data, which helps them understand intricate details.

The Introduction of architecture like convolutional neural networks (CNNs) and recurrent neural networks (RNNs) was a major advancement in deep learning. CNNs are great for image processing, while RNNs are good for sequential data, like time series and language.

1.7.2 Breakthroughs in Image and Speech Recognition

Deep learning achieved great success in areas like image and speech recognition. CNNs revolutionized computer vision, allowing AI to perform as well as humans in tasks like object detection and facial recognition. The ability of CNNs to automatically learn features from images reduced the need for manual feature extraction, which had been a bottleneck in traditional computer vision.

Similarly, advancements in RNNs and long short-term memory (LSTM) networks transformed natural language processing (NLP). These architectures allowed for more accurate speech recognition and language translation, leading to applications like real-time translation services and voice assistants. The combination of large datasets and powerful deep learning models led to breakthroughs that were previously thought impossible.

1.7.3 The Role of GPUs

The rise of graphics processing units (GPUs) was crucial for deep learning. Originally designed for video games, GPUs turned out to be great for the parallel processing needed to train deep neural networks. This allowed researchers to train larger models on huge datasets in much less time, speeding up AI development.

The parallel architecture of GPUs allowed them to perform thousands of operations at once, making them ideal for the math needed in deep learning. This hardware revolution made powerful computing resources more accessible, allowing more researchers and developers to experiment with complex models and large datasets.

1.7.4 Open Source and Collaboration

The deep learning revolution was also fueled by the open-source movement, which made powerful AI tools and libraries available to everyone. Tools like TensorFlow, PyTorch, and Keras made AI research more accessible, allowing a wider community to contribute to advancements. These tools provided user-friendly interfaces and pre-built functions that simplified the process of building and training deep learning models.

Collaborative efforts, like competitions on platforms like Kaggle, encouraged innovation and knowledge sharing, leading to rapid progress in AI. This collaborative spirit fostered a vibrant community where researchers could build on each other's work, leading to rapid improvements in algorithms and models.

1.8 AI in the 21st Century: Today's Trends and Uses

1.8.1 AI in Business

As we moved into the 21st century, AI started to appear in many industries, changing how businesses operate. Companies in areas like healthcare, finance, retail, and manufacturing began using AI to improve efficiency, customer experience, and innovation. For example, AI helps doctors diagnose diseases more accurately, and in finance, AI helps manage risks and optimize investments.

In retail, AI personalizes shopping experiences, leading to more sales and happier customers. In manufacturing, AI optimizes supply chains and predicts maintenance needs, reducing downtime and costs. Using AI in business has become a key way for companies to stay competitive.

1.8.2 AI in Everyday Life

AI has become a part of our daily lives. Virtual assistants like Siri, Alexa, and Google Assistant use natural language processing to understand and respond to our questions, making technology more accessible. These assistants use machine learning to get better over time, providing more accurate and relevant information.

Recommendation systems on platforms like Netflix and Amazon suggest content and products based on our preferences, making our experiences more enjoyable. Social media platforms use AI to curate news feeds and target ads, shaping how we interact with online content.

1.8.3 Ethical Issues

As AI continues to grow, ethical considerations have become very important. Issues like bias in algorithms, data privacy, and job displacement raise important questions about how we should use AI responsibly. Researchers, policymakers, and industry leaders are focusing on developing rules and guidelines to ensure AI is used ethically and for the benefit of society.

The potential for bias in AI systems, which comes from the data used to train them, has received a lot of attention. Ensuring fairness and transparency in AI decisions is crucial for building trust. Also, the impact of AI on jobs requires us to think about retraining and helping people find new jobs.

1.9 Conclusion

The rise of AI is a testament to human creativity and the constant pursuit of knowledge. From its early days in the 1950s to today's deep learning and data-driven applications, AI has come a long way. As we look to the future, it's important to use AI to improve our lives while being careful about the ethical issues. The AI journey is far from over, and its potential is limited only by our imagination and commitment to responsible innovation.

II

The Potential of AI:

Transforming Our Lives

Artificial Intelligence (AI) is no longer a concept confined to the realms of science fiction; it is a transformative force that is reshaping our daily lives, industries, and the very fabric of society. From personal assistants that streamline our schedules to self-driving cars that promise safer commutes, AI is poised to revolutionize how we interact with technology and each other. This exploration delves into the multifaceted potential of AI, examining its applications, benefits, challenges, and the ethical considerations that accompany its integration into our lives.

1. AI-Powered Personal Assistants

1.1 Enhancing Daily Productivity

AI-powered personal assistants, such as Siri, Google Assistant, and Alexa, have become ubiquitous in our lives. These digital companions are designed to help us manage our time and tasks more efficiently. By utilizing natural language processing (NLP) and machine learning algorithms, these assistants can understand and respond to voice commands, making it easier for users to schedule appointments, set reminders, and even control smart home devices.

Imagine waking up in the morning and asking your personal assistant to provide a summary of your day. It can pull information from your calendar, suggest the best route to work based on real-time traffic data, and even remind you to pick up groceries on your way home. This level of integration not only saves time but also reduces the cognitive load on individuals, allowing them to focus on more important tasks.

1.2 Personalized Recommendations

Beyond basic task management, AI personal assistants can learn from user behavior to provide personalized recommendations. For instance, they can suggest restaurants based on your dining history, recommend movies aligned with your tastes, or even curate playlists that match your mood. This personalization enhances user experience and fosters a deeper connection between individuals and technology.

1.3 Accessibility and Inclusivity

AI personal assistants also play a crucial role in enhancing accessibility for individuals with disabilities. Voice-activated technology allows those with mobility impairments to interact with devices and access information without physical barriers. For individuals with visual impairments, AI can read text aloud, describe images, and even navigate environments, making technology more inclusive.

2. AI in Transportation: Self-Driving Cars

2.1 The Promise of Autonomous Vehicles

Self-driving cars represent one of the most exciting applications of AI technology. By leveraging advanced sensors, machine learning algorithms, and real-time data analysis, autonomous vehicles can navigate complex environments, make split-second decisions, and communicate with other vehicles and infrastructure. The potential benefits of self-driving cars are vast, including reduced traffic accidents, decreased congestion, and increased mobility for those unable to drive.

2.2 Safety and Efficiency

One of the primary advantages of self-driving cars is their potential to enhance road safety. According to the National Highway Traffic Safety Administration (NHTSA), human error is a factor in approximately 94% of traffic accidents. By removing the human element, AI can significantly reduce the likelihood of accidents caused by distractions, fatigue, or impaired judgment.

Moreover, self-driving cars can optimize traffic flow by communicating with each other and adjusting their speeds accordingly. This coordination can lead to smoother commutes, reduced travel times, and lower emissions, contributing to a more sustainable transportation system.

2.3 Challenges and Considerations

Despite the promise of self-driving cars, several challenges remain. Regulatory frameworks need to be established to ensure safety and accountability. Ethical dilemmas also arise, such as how an autonomous vehicle should react in unavoidable accident scenarios. Public acceptance and trust in this technology will be crucial for its widespread adoption.

3. AI in Healthcare: Revolutionizing Medical Diagnosis

3.1 Enhancing Diagnostic Accuracy

AI's impact on healthcare is profound, particularly in the realm of medical diagnosis. Machine learning algorithms can analyze vast amounts of medical data, including patient records, imaging studies, and genetic information, to assist healthcare professionals in making more accurate diagnoses. For instance, AI systems can identify patterns in medical images that may be imperceptible to the human eye, leading to earlier detection of conditions such as cancer.

3.2 Personalized Treatment Plans

AI can also facilitate the development of personalized treatment plans tailored to individual patients. By analyzing genetic data and treatment outcomes, AI can help doctors identify the most effective therapies for specific patients, minimizing trial-and-error approaches and improving overall patient outcomes.

3.3 Predictive Analytics

In addition to diagnosis and treatment, AI can play a crucial role in predictive analytics. By analyzing historical data, AI can identify trends and risk factors, enabling healthcare providers to intervene proactively. For example, AI can predict which patients are at risk of developing chronic conditions, allowing for early intervention and preventive care.

3.4 Ethical Considerations in Healthcare AI

While the potential benefits of AI in healthcare are significant, ethical considerations must be addressed. Issues related to data privacy, algorithmic bias, and the need for transparency in AI decision-making processes are critical. Ensuring that AI systems are developed and implemented responsibly is essential to maintaining trust in healthcare technologies.

4. AI in Education: Personalized Learning Experiences

4.1 Tailoring Education to Individual Needs

AI has the potential to transform education by providing personalized learning experiences. Adaptive learning platforms can analyze student performance in real-time and adjust the curriculum to meet individual needs. This approach allows students to learn at their own pace, ensuring that they grasp concepts before moving on to more complex topics.

4.2 Intelligent Tutoring Systems

Intelligent tutoring systems powered by AI can offer additional support to students outside the classroom. These systems can provide instant feedback, answer questions, and guide learners through challenging material. By simulating one-on-one tutoring, AI can help bridge the gap for students who may struggle in traditional classroom settings.

4.3 Enhancing Teacher Effectiveness

AI can also assist educators by automating administrative tasks, such as grading and attendance tracking. This automation frees up teachers to focus on instruction and student engagement. Additionally, AI can provide insights into student performance, helping educators identify areas where students may need extra support.

4.4 Challenges in Educational AI

Despite its potential, the integration of AI in education faces challenges, including concerns about data privacy and the digital divide. Ensuring equitable access to AI-driven educational tools is crucial to prevent widening the gap between students with different socioeconomic backgrounds.

5. AI in Business: Streamlining Operations

5.1 Automating Routine Tasks

In the business world, AI is streamlining operations by automating routine tasks. From data entry to customer service inquiries, AI-powered chatbots can handle a variety of functions, allowing employees to focus on more strategic initiatives. This automation not only increases efficiency but also reduces operational costs.

5.2 Data-Driven Decision Making

AI enables businesses to harness the power of data analytics for informed decision-making. By analyzing market trends, customer behavior, and operational performance, AI can provide valuable insights that drive strategic planning. Companies can leverage these insights to optimize marketing campaigns, improve product offerings, and enhance customer experiences.

5.3 Enhancing Customer Experience

AI can significantly enhance customer experience through personalized interactions. By analysing customer data, businesses can tailor their marketing efforts and product recommendations to individual preferences. This level of personalization fosters customer loyalty and satisfaction.

5.4 Ethical Considerations in Business AI

As businesses increasingly rely on AI, ethical considerations must be addressed. Issues such as data privacy, algorithmic bias, and the potential for job displacement are critical. Companies must navigate these challenges responsibly to build trust with consumers and employees.

6. The Future of AI: Opportunities and Challenges

6.1 The Evolving Landscape of AI Technology

The future of AI holds immense promise, with advancements in machine learning, natural language processing, and robotics. As technology continues to evolve, new applications will emerge, further integrating AI into our daily lives. The potential for innovation is vast, spanning industries from agriculture to finance.

6.2 Addressing Ethical and Societal Implications

As AI becomes more pervasive, addressing ethical and societal implications will be paramount. Policymakers, technologists, and ethicists must collaborate to establish guidelines that ensure responsible AI development and deployment. This collaboration will help mitigate risks associated with bias, privacy, and accountability.

6.3 Preparing for an AI-Driven Workforce

The rise of AI will inevitably reshape the workforce. While some jobs may be displaced, new opportunities will emerge in AI development, maintenance, and oversight. Preparing the workforce for this transition through education and reskilling initiatives will be essential to harnessing the full potential of AI.

6.4 Conclusion: Embracing the AI Revolution

The potential of AI to transform our lives is undeniable. From enhancing productivity and safety to revolutionizing healthcare and education, AI is poised to reshape the future. However, as we embrace this technological revolution, it is crucial to navigate the challenges and ethical considerations that accompany it. By fostering responsible AI development and ensuring equitable access, we can harness the power of AI to create a better, more inclusive future for all. ## 7. AI in Finance: Transforming Financial Services

7. Risk Assessment and Management

In the finance sector, AI is revolutionizing risk assessment and management. Machine learning algorithms can analyse vast datasets to identify potential risks and predict market trends. Financial institutions can leverage these insights to make informed decisions, manage portfolios more effectively, and mitigate risks associated with lending and investment.

7.1 Fraud Detection

AI plays a critical role in enhancing security within financial services. By analyzing transaction patterns and identifying anomalies, AI systems can detect fraudulent activities in real-time. This proactive approach not only protects consumers but also helps financial institutions minimize losses and maintain trust.

7.2 Personalized Financial Services

AI enables financial institutions to offer personalized services tailored to individual customer needs. By analyzing customer data, banks can provide customized financial advice, investment strategies, and product recommendations. This level of personalization enhances customer satisfaction and loyalty, as clients feel understood and valued.

7.3 Regulatory Compliance

The financial industry is heavily regulated, and AI can assist in ensuring compliance with various regulations. AI systems can monitor transactions and flag any activities that may violate regulatory standards, helping institutions avoid costly penalties and maintain their reputations.

8. AI in Agriculture: Enhancing Food Production

8.1 Precision Farming

AI is transforming agriculture through precision farming techniques. By utilizing data from sensors, drones, and satellite imagery, farmers can monitor crop health, soil conditions, and weather patterns. This data-driven approach allows for more efficient resource allocation, optimizing yields while minimizing waste.

8.2 Pest and Disease Management

AI can also aid in pest and disease management by analyzing data to predict outbreaks and recommend preventive measures. Machine learning algorithms can identify patterns in crop health and environmental conditions, enabling farmers to take proactive steps to protect their crops.

8.3 Supply Chain Optimization

AI enhances the agricultural supply chain by improving logistics and distribution. By analyzing demand patterns and inventory levels, AI can optimize delivery routes and schedules, reducing costs and ensuring that fresh produce reaches consumers in a timely manner.

9. AI in Entertainment: Redefining Content Creation

9.1 Content Recommendation Systems

In the entertainment industry, AI is reshaping how content is created and consumed. Streaming platforms like Netflix and Spotify utilize AI-driven recommendation systems to analyze user preferences and viewing habits. This personalization enhances user engagement and satisfaction, as consumers discover content tailored to their tastes.

9.2 AI-Generated Content

AI is also making strides in content creation itself. Algorithms can generate music, write scripts, and even create visual art. While this raises questions about creativity and authorship, it also opens new avenues for collaboration between humans and machines in the creative process.

9.3 Enhancing User Experience

AI enhances user experience in gaming and virtual reality by creating more immersive environments. AI-driven characters can adapt to player behavior, providing a dynamic and engaging experience. This level of interactivity elevates entertainment to new heights, captivating audiences in unprecedented ways.

10. AI in Environmental Sustainability: Addressing Climate Change

10.1 Climate Modeling and Prediction

AI is playing a vital role in addressing climate change by improving climate modeling and prediction. Machine learning algorithms can analyze vast datasets related to weather patterns, greenhouse gas emissions, and land use changes. This information helps scientists and policymakers make informed decisions to mitigate climate impacts.

10.2 Resource Management

AI can optimize resource management in various sectors, including energy and water. Smart grids powered by AI can balance energy supply and demand, reducing waste and promoting the use of renewable energy sources. Similarly, AI can enhance water management by predicting usage patterns and identifying leaks in infrastructure.

10.3 Biodiversity Conservation

AI technologies are being employed in biodiversity conservation efforts. By analyzing data from camera traps and satellite imagery, AI can monitor wildlife populations and track changes in ecosystems. This information is crucial for developing effective conservation strategies and protecting endangered species.

11. AI in Cybersecurity: Safeguarding Digital Assets

11.1 Threat Detection and Response

As cyber threats become increasingly sophisticated, AI is essential in enhancing cybersecurity measures. AI systems can analyze network traffic and user behavior to detect anomalies indicative of potential breaches. This proactive approach allows organizations to respond swiftly to threats, minimizing damage.

11.2 Automated Security Protocols

AI can automate security protocols, ensuring that systems are continuously monitored and updated. By leveraging machine learning, organizations can adapt their security measures in real-time, staying ahead of emerging threats and vulnerabilities.

11.3 User Authentication

AI enhances user authentication processes through biometric recognition and behavioral analysis. By analyzing patterns in user behavior, AI can identify potential security risks and prevent unauthorized access to sensitive information.

12. Conclusion: The Path Forward

The potential of AI to transform various sectors is immense, offering innovative solutions to complex challenges. As we continue to explore the capabilities of AI, it is essential to address the ethical, societal, and regulatory implications that accompany its integration. By fostering collaboration among stakeholders, including technologists, policymakers, and ethicists, we can create a framework that promotes responsible AI development. This collaborative approach will help ensure that the benefits of AI are distributed equitably across society, minimizing risks and maximizing opportunities.

12.1 Emphasizing Education and Awareness

To fully harness the potential of AI, it is crucial to invest in education and awareness initiatives. By equipping individuals with the knowledge and skills necessary to navigate an AI-driven world, we can empower them to engage with technology responsibly. Educational programs should focus on digital literacy, ethical considerations, and the implications of AI in various fields.

12.2 Encouraging Innovation and Research

Continued investment in research and innovation is vital for advancing AI technologies. Governments, academic institutions, and private organizations should collaborate to fund research initiatives that explore new applications of AI, address existing challenges, and develop ethical guidelines for its use. This commitment to innovation will drive progress and ensure that AI remains a force for good.

12.3 Building Trust Through Transparency

Transparency is key to building trust in AI systems. Organizations must be open about how AI algorithms function, the data they use, and the decision-making processes involved. By providing clear explanations and ensuring accountability, stakeholders can foster public confidence in AI technologies.

12.4 Conclusion: A Collective Responsibility

As we stand on the brink of an AI-driven future, it is our collective responsibility to shape its trajectory. By embracing the potential of AI while addressing the ethical and societal implications, we can create a future where technology enhances our lives, promotes inclusivity, and drives sustainable progress. The journey ahead will require collaboration, innovation, and a commitment to responsible practices, ensuring that AI serves as a tool for positive change in our world.

13. AI in Retail: Transforming the Shopping Experience

13.1 Personalized Shopping Experiences

AI is revolutionizing the retail sector by creating personalized shopping experiences for consumers. Retailers can analyze customer data to understand preferences and shopping behaviors, allowing them to tailor product recommendations and marketing strategies. This level of personalization not only enhances customer satisfaction but also drives sales by presenting consumers with products they are more likely to purchase.

13.2 Inventory Management

AI can significantly improve inventory management by predicting demand and optimizing stock levels. Machine learning algorithms analyze historical sales data, seasonal trends, and market conditions to forecast inventory needs accurately. This predictive capability helps retailers reduce excess stock, minimize waste, and ensure that popular items are always available for customers.

13.3 Enhancing Customer Service

AI-powered chatbots and virtual assistants are transforming customer service in retail. These tools can handle inquiries, provide product information, and assist with order tracking, offering customers immediate support. By automating these interactions, retailers can improve response times and free up human agents to focus on more complex issues.

13.4 Visual Search and Augmented Reality

AI technologies such as visual search and augmented reality (AR) are enhancing the shopping experience. Visual search allows customers to upload images of products they are interested in, and AI can identify similar items available for purchase. AR applications enable customers to visualize products in their own space, such as trying on clothes virtually or seeing how furniture fits in their home, making the shopping experience more interactive and engaging.

14. AI in Human Resources: Streamlining Recruitment and Employee Management

14.1 Recruitment Automation

AI is streamlining the recruitment process by automating candidate screening and selection. Machine learning algorithms can analyze resumes and applications to identify the best candidates based on specific criteria, reducing the time and effort required for human recruiters. This automation allows HR professionals to focus on building relationships with candidates and enhancing the overall hiring experience.

14.2 Employee Engagement and Retention

AI can also play a crucial role in employee engagement and retention. By analyzing employee feedback, performance data, and engagement surveys, AI systems can identify trends and areas for improvement. This information enables organizations to implement targeted strategies to enhance workplace culture, boost morale, and reduce turnover rates.

14.3 Training and Development

AI-driven platforms can personalize training and development programs for employees. By assessing individual learning styles and performance metrics, these systems can recommend tailored training modules that align with employees' career goals and skill gaps. This personalized approach fosters continuous learning and professional growth within organizations.

15. AI in Smart Cities: Enhancing Urban Living

15.1 Intelligent Infrastructure

AI is integral to the development of smart cities, where technology is used to enhance urban living. Intelligent infrastructure, powered by AI, can optimize traffic management, reduce energy consumption, and improve public safety. For example, AI algorithms can analyze traffic patterns to adjust traffic signals in real-time, reducing congestion and improving commute times.

15.2 Public Safety and Emergency Response

AI technologies can enhance public safety by analyzing data from surveillance cameras, social media, and emergency calls. Predictive analytics can help law enforcement agencies identify potential crime hotspots and allocate resources more effectively. Additionally, AI can assist in emergency response by analyzing real-time data to coordinate rescue efforts during natural disasters or public emergencies.

15.3 Sustainable Urban Planning

AI can support sustainable urban planning by analyzing environmental data and predicting the impact of urban development on ecosystems. This information can guide policymakers in making informed decisions that balance growth with environmental preservation, ensuring that cities remain livable for future generations.

16. AI in Manufacturing: Optimizing Production Processes

16.1 Predictive Maintenance

In manufacturing, AI is enhancing operational efficiency through predictive maintenance. By analyzing data from machinery and equipment, AI can predict when maintenance is needed, reducing downtime and preventing costly breakdowns. This proactive approach ensures that production processes run smoothly and efficiently.

16.2 Quality Control

AI technologies can improve quality control by analyzing products during the manufacturing process. Machine learning algorithms can identify defects and inconsistencies in real-time, allowing manufacturers to address issues immediately. This capability not only enhances product quality but also reduces waste and rework costs.

16.3 Supply Chain Optimization

AI can optimize supply chain management by analyzing data related to inventory levels, supplier performance, and market demand. This analysis enables manufacturers to make informed decisions about sourcing materials, managing logistics, and responding to fluctuations in demand, ultimately improving overall supply chain efficiency.

17. AI in Telecommunications: Enhancing Connectivity

17.1 Network Optimization

AI is transforming the telecommunications industry by optimizing network performance. Machine learning algorithms can analyze network traffic patterns and user behavior to identify areas for improvement. This optimization ensures that users experience reliable connectivity and high-quality service.

17.2 Customer Support Automation

Telecommunications companies are leveraging AI to automate customer support processes. AI-powered chatbots can handle routine inquiries, troubleshoot issues, and provide account information, allowing human agents to focus on more complex customer needs. This automation enhances customer satisfaction by providing quick and efficient service.

17.3 Predictive Maintenance in Networks

AI can also play a crucial role in predictive maintenance for telecommunications networks. By analyzing data from network equipment, AI systems can predict potential failures and recommend maintenance before issues arise. This proactive approach minimizes downtime and ensures uninterrupted service for customers.

17.4 Enhancing User Experience

AI technologies can enhance user experience by personalizing services and recommendations. For instance, telecom providers can analyze customer usage patterns to offer tailored plans and services that meet individual needs. This level of personalization fosters customer loyalty and satisfaction.

18. AI in Logistics: Streamlining Supply Chain Operations

18.1 Route Optimization

AI is revolutionizing logistics by optimizing delivery routes. Machine learning algorithms can analyze traffic patterns, weather conditions, and delivery schedules to determine the most efficient routes for transportation. This optimization reduces fuel consumption, lowers costs, and improves delivery times.

18.2 Inventory Management and Forecasting

AI can enhance inventory management in logistics by predicting demand and optimizing stock levels. By analyzing historical data and market trends, AI systems can forecast inventory needs, ensuring that warehouses are stocked appropriately and reducing the risk of overstocking or stockouts.

18.3 Real-Time Tracking and Visibility

AI technologies enable real-time tracking of shipments, providing visibility throughout the supply chain. This transparency allows logistics companies to monitor the status of deliveries, anticipate delays, and communicate effectively with customers, enhancing overall service quality.

19. AI in Insurance: Transforming Risk Assessment and Claims Processing

19.1 Automated Underwriting

In the insurance industry, AI is streamlining the underwriting process by automating risk assessment. Machine learning algorithms can analyze vast amounts of data, including customer profiles and historical claims, to determine risk levels and set premiums more accurately. This automation speeds up the underwriting process and improves accuracy.

19.2 Fraud Detection in Claims

AI plays a critical role in detecting fraudulent claims in the insurance sector. By analyzing patterns in claims data, AI systems can identify anomalies that may indicate fraud. This proactive approach helps insurers minimize losses and maintain the integrity of their operations.

19.3 Personalized Insurance Products

AI enables insurance companies to offer personalized products tailored to individual customer needs. By analyzing customer data, insurers can create customized policies that align with specific risks and preferences, enhancing customer satisfaction and loyalty.

20. AI in Real Estate: Enhancing Property Management and Sales

20.1 Property Valuation and Market Analysis

AI is transforming the real estate industry by improving property valuation and market analysis. Machine learning algorithms can analyze historical sales data, market trends, and property features to provide accurate valuations. This capability helps buyers and sellers make informed decisions in the real estate market.

20.2 Virtual Tours and Augmented Reality

AI technologies enable virtual tours and augmented reality experiences in real estate. Potential buyers can explore properties remotely, visualizing spaces and layouts without physically visiting. This innovation enhances the buying experience and expands the reach of real estate listings.

20.3 Predictive Analytics for Investment

AI can assist real estate investors by providing predictive analytics on market trends and property values. By analyzing data from various sources, AI systems can identify emerging markets and investment opportunities, helping investors make strategic decisions.

21. AI in Sports: Enhancing Performance and Fan Engagement

21.1 Performance Analysis

AI is revolutionizing sports by providing in-depth performance analysis for athletes and teams. Machine learning algorithms can analyze game footage, player statistics, and training data to identify strengths and weaknesses. This analysis helps coaches and athletes make data-driven decisions to enhance performance.

21.2 Fan Engagement and Experience

AI technologies are enhancing fan engagement through personalized experiences. Sports organizations can analyze fan data to tailor marketing efforts, offer customized content, and create interactive experiences during games. This level of engagement fosters a deeper connection between fans and their favorite teams.

21.3 Injury Prevention and Recovery

AI can play a crucial role in injury prevention and recovery in sports. By analyzing player biomechanics and training loads, AI systems can identify risk factors for injuries and recommend personalized training regimens. This proactive approach helps athletes stay healthy and perform at their best.

22. AI in Space Exploration: Expanding Our Horizons

22.1 Autonomous Spacecraft

AI is transforming space exploration by enabling autonomous spacecraft to navigate and make decisions in real-time. Machine learning algorithms can analyze data from sensors and cameras, allowing spacecraft to adapt to changing conditions and optimize their missions.

22.2 Data Analysis in Astronomy

AI technologies are enhancing data analysis in astronomy by processing vast amounts of data from telescopes and satellites. Machine learning algorithms can identify celestial objects, analyze patterns, and contribute to discoveries in astrophysics, expanding our understanding of the universe.

22.3 Supporting Human Exploration

AI can support human exploration of space by assisting astronauts in various tasks. From monitoring health metrics to providing real-time data analysis, AI can enhance the safety and efficiency of missions. By automating routine tasks, AI allows astronauts to focus on critical decision-making and problem-solving, ultimately improving mission outcomes.

23. AI in Disaster Management: Enhancing Response and Recovery

23.1 Predictive Analytics for Disaster Preparedness

AI plays a vital role in disaster management by utilizing predictive analytics to assess risks and prepare for potential disasters. By analyzing historical data, weather patterns, and geographical information, AI can forecast the likelihood of events such as floods, earthquakes, and hurricanes. This information enables governments and organizations to develop effective response plans and allocate resources efficiently.

23.2 Real-Time Monitoring and Response

During disasters, AI technologies can facilitate real-time monitoring and response efforts. Drones equipped with AI can assess damage, locate survivors, and deliver supplies to affected areas. Additionally, AI can analyze social media data to identify urgent needs and coordinate relief efforts, ensuring that help reaches those in need promptly.

23.3 Post-Disaster Recovery

AI can assist in post-disaster recovery by analyzing data to evaluate the impact of disasters on communities. This analysis helps policymakers understand the extent of damage and prioritize recovery efforts. Furthermore, AI can support rebuilding initiatives by identifying areas that require immediate attention and resources.

24. AI in Mental Health: Supporting Well-Being

24.1 AI-Powered Mental Health Apps

AI is making strides in mental health support through the development of AI-powered applications. These apps can provide users with personalized coping strategies, mood tracking, and access to resources. By analyzing user data, AI can offer tailored recommendations that promote mental well-being.

24.2 Virtual Therapy and Support

AI technologies are also being integrated into virtual therapy platforms, allowing individuals to access mental health support from the comfort of their homes. AI chatbots can engage users in conversations, providing immediate support and guidance. While not a replacement for human therapists, these tools can complement traditional therapy and increase accessibility.

24.3 Early Detection of Mental Health Issues

AI can aid in the early detection of mental health issues by analyzing patterns in user behavior and communication. By identifying signs of distress or changes in mood, AI systems can alert users to seek professional help, potentially preventing more severe mental health crises.

25. AI in Fashion: Redefining Trends and Consumer Engagement

25.1 Trend Forecasting

AI is transforming the fashion industry by enhancing trend forecasting capabilities. Machine learning algorithms can analyze social media, online searches, and consumer behavior to predict emerging fashion trends. This data-driven approach allows brands to stay ahead of the curve and align their collections with consumer preferences.

25.2 Virtual Fitting Rooms

AI technologies are revolutionizing the shopping experience in fashion through virtual fitting rooms. Customers can use augmented reality to try on clothes virtually, allowing them to visualize how items will look without physically trying them on. This innovation enhances customer satisfaction and reduces return rates.

25.3 Sustainable Fashion Practices

AI can also contribute to sustainable fashion practices by optimizing supply chains and reducing waste. By analyzing data on production processes and consumer demand, AI can help brands make informed decisions that minimize environmental impact and promote ethical practices.

26. AI in Gaming: Creating Immersive Experiences

26.1 Dynamic Game Environments

AI is enhancing the gaming industry by creating dynamic and immersive environments. Machine learning algorithms can adapt game scenarios based on player behavior, providing a unique experience for each user. This level of interactivity keeps players engaged and encourages exploration.

26.2 Non-Player Character (NPC) Behavior

AI technologies are improving the behavior of non-player characters (NPCs) in games. By utilizing advanced algorithms, NPCs can exhibit realistic behaviors and respond intelligently to player actions. This realism enhances gameplay and creates a more engaging experience for players.

26.3 Personalized Gaming Experiences

AI can analyze player preferences and performance to offer personalized gaming experiences. By tailoring challenges and rewards to individual players, AI ensures that games remain enjoyable and motivating, catering to a wide range of skill levels.

27. AI in Music: Transforming the Industry

27.1 Music Composition and Production

AI is making waves in the music industry by assisting in composition and production. Algorithms can analyze existing music to generate new compositions, providing artists with inspiration and creative ideas. This collaboration between humans and machines is reshaping the creative process.

27.2 Personalized Music Recommendations

Streaming platforms are leveraging AI to provide personalized music recommendations based on user listening habits. By analyzing data, AI can curate playlists that align with individual tastes, enhancing the overall listening experience and fostering discovery.

27.3 Enhancing Live Performances

AI technologies are also being integrated into live performances, enhancing the audience experience. From interactive visuals to real-time sound manipulation, AI can create immersive environments that captivate concert-goers and elevate the overall performance.

28. AI in Language Translation: Bridging Communication Gaps

28.1 Real-Time Language Translation

AI is revolutionizing language translation by providing real-time translation services that break down communication barriers. Machine learning algorithms can analyze vast amounts of text data to improve translation accuracy and fluency. This capability is particularly beneficial in a globalized world where effective communication across languages is essential for business, travel, and cultural exchange.

28.2 Contextual Understanding

One of the significant advancements in AI-driven translation is the ability to understand context. Traditional translation methods often struggled with idiomatic expressions and cultural nuances. However, AI systems can now consider the context in which words and phrases are used, resulting in translations that are not only accurate but also culturally relevant. This improvement enhances the user experience and fosters better understanding between speakers of different languages.

28.3 Applications in Various Sectors

AI-powered translation tools are being utilized across various sectors, including education, healthcare, and customer service. In education, these tools facilitate learning by providing students with access to resources in their native languages. In healthcare, they enable medical professionals to communicate effectively with patients who speak different languages, ensuring that critical information is conveyed accurately. In customer service, AI translation tools help businesses engage with a global audience, providing support in multiple languages.

28.4 Future Prospects

As AI technology continues to evolve, the future of language translation looks promising. Ongoing advancements in natural language processing and machine learning will likely lead to even more sophisticated translation systems capable of handling complex linguistic challenges. This progress will further enhance global communication, making it easier for individuals and organizations to connect across language barriers.

29. AI in Social Media: Shaping Online Interactions

29.1 Content Moderation

AI is playing a crucial role in content moderation on social media platforms. Machine learning algorithms can analyze user-generated content to identify and flag inappropriate or harmful material. This capability helps maintain a safe online environment by reducing the spread of misinformation, hate speech, and other harmful content.

29.2 Personalized User Experiences

Social media platforms leverage AI to create personalized user experiences. By analyzing user behavior, preferences, and interactions, AI algorithms can curate content feeds that align with individual interests. This personalization enhances user engagement and satisfaction, encouraging users to spend more time on the platform.

29.3 Influencer Marketing

AI is transforming influencer marketing by providing brands with data-driven insights into influencer performance and audience engagement. By analyzing metrics such as reach, engagement rates, and audience demographics, AI helps brands identify the most effective influencers for their campaigns, optimizing marketing strategies and maximizing return on investment.

30. AI in Customer Relationship Management (CRM): Enhancing Business Interactions

30.1 Data-Driven Insights

AI is revolutionizing customer relationship management by providing businesses with data-driven insights into customer behavior and preferences. By analyzing customer interactions, purchase history, and feedback, AI systems can identify trends and patterns that inform marketing strategies and product development.

30.2 Predictive Customer Analytics

AI can enhance CRM systems through predictive analytics, enabling businesses to anticipate customer needs and preferences. By analyzing historical data, AI can forecast future behavior, allowing companies to tailor their offerings and improve customer satisfaction.

30.3 Automation of Customer Interactions

AI-powered chatbots and virtual assistants are streamlining customer interactions by automating routine inquiries and support tasks. This automation not only improves response times but also allows human agents to focus on more complex issues, enhancing overall customer service quality.

31. AI in Public Health: Improving Community Well-Being

31.1 Disease Surveillance

AI is playing a vital role in public health by enhancing disease surveillance and outbreak prediction. Machine learning algorithms can analyze data from various sources, including social media, healthcare records, and environmental factors, to identify potential outbreaks and monitor disease spread. This capability enables public health officials to respond proactively and allocate resources effectively.

31.2 Health Education and Promotion

AI technologies can support health education and promotion efforts by analyzing community health data and identifying areas of concern. By tailoring educational campaigns to specific populations, AI can help raise awareness about health issues and promote preventive measures, ultimately improving community well-being.

31.3 Telehealth Services

The integration of AI in telehealth services is transforming healthcare delivery. AI-powered platforms can facilitate remote consultations, monitor patient health, and provide personalized recommendations. This accessibility enhances healthcare delivery, particularly for individuals in underserved areas or those with mobility challenges.

32. AI in Ethics and Governance: Navigating Challenges

32.1 Ethical Frameworks for AI Development

As AI technology continues to advance, establishing ethical frameworks for its development and deployment is crucial. Policymakers, technologists, and ethicists must collaborate to create guidelines that address issues such as bias, transparency, and accountability. These frameworks will help ensure that AI systems are developed responsibly and serve the public good.

32.2 Governance and Regulation

Governance and regulation of AI technologies are essential to mitigate risks and protect individuals' rights. Governments and regulatory bodies must establish policies that promote responsible AI use while encouraging innovation. This balance is vital to foster an environment where AI can thrive while ensuring that ethical considerations are prioritized.

32.3 Public Engagement and Awareness

Engaging the public in discussions about AI ethics and governance is essential for building trust and understanding. By raising awareness about the implications of AI technologies, stakeholders can encourage informed dialogue and participation in shaping policies that govern AI use. Public input can help identify concerns and expectations, leading to more effective and inclusive governance frameworks.

32.4 Addressing Algorithmic Bias

One of the significant challenges in AI ethics is addressing algorithmic bias. AI systems can inadvertently perpetuate existing biases present in training data, leading to unfair outcomes. It is crucial to implement strategies for identifying and mitigating bias in AI algorithms, ensuring that these systems operate fairly and equitably across diverse populations.

33. AI in Climate Change Mitigation: A Collaborative Approach

33.1 AI for Renewable Energy

AI is playing a pivotal role in advancing renewable energy technologies. By optimizing energy production and consumption, AI can enhance the efficiency of solar panels, wind turbines, and other renewable sources. Machine learning algorithms can analyze weather patterns and energy demand, enabling better integration of renewable energy into existing grids.

33.2 Carbon Footprint Reduction

AI can assist organizations in reducing their carbon footprints by analyzing operational data and identifying areas for improvement. By optimizing processes and resource allocation, AI can help businesses implement sustainable practices that minimize environmental impact.

33.3 Collaborative Efforts for Climate Action

Addressing climate change requires collaboration among governments, businesses, and communities. AI can facilitate these efforts by providing data-driven insights that inform policy decisions and promote sustainable practices. By leveraging AI technologies, stakeholders can work together to develop innovative solutions that combat climate change effectively.

34. AI in Humanitarian Aid: Enhancing Response Efforts

34.1 Disaster Relief Coordination

AI is transforming humanitarian aid by improving disaster relief coordination. Machine learning algorithms can analyze data from various sources to assess needs and allocate resources effectively during crises. This capability enables organizations to respond more quickly and efficiently, ultimately saving lives.

34.2 Predictive Analytics for Vulnerable Populations

AI can enhance the identification of vulnerable populations in need of assistance. By analyzing demographic data and social indicators, AI systems can predict which communities are at higher risk during disasters, allowing aid organizations to target their efforts more effectively.

34.3 Enhancing Communication in Crisis Situations

AI technologies can improve communication during humanitarian crises by analyzing social media and other communication channels. By identifying urgent needs and public sentiment, organizations can tailor their messaging and outreach efforts, ensuring that assistance reaches those who need it most.

35. AI in Transportation Logistics: Improving Efficiency

35.1 Fleet Management Optimization

AI is revolutionizing transportation logistics by optimizing fleet management. Machine learning algorithms can analyze data related to vehicle performance, fuel consumption, and route efficiency, enabling companies to make data-driven decisions that enhance operational efficiency.

35.2 Last-Mile Delivery Solutions

AI technologies are improving last-mile delivery solutions by optimizing routes and delivery schedules. By analyzing traffic patterns and customer preferences, AI can enhance the efficiency of delivery operations, reducing costs and improving customer satisfaction.

35.3 Autonomous Delivery Vehicles

The rise of autonomous delivery vehicles is another significant development in transportation logistics. AI-powered drones and self-driving vehicles can streamline delivery processes, reducing reliance on human drivers and enhancing efficiency in the supply chain.

36. AI in Telecommunications Infrastructure: Future Innovations

36.1 5G Network Optimization

AI is playing a crucial role in optimizing 5G networks, enabling faster and more reliable connectivity. Machine learning algorithms can analyze network performance data to identify areas for improvement, ensuring that users experience seamless connectivity.

36.2 Enhancing Network Security

As telecommunications networks become more complex, AI is essential for enhancing network security. AI systems can monitor network traffic for anomalies and potential threats, enabling proactive measures to protect sensitive data and maintain service integrity.

36.3 Customer Experience Enhancement

AI technologies are enhancing customer experience in telecommunications by providing personalized services and support. By analyzing customer data, telecom providers can tailor offerings and improve service delivery, fostering customer loyalty and satisfaction.

37. AI in Urban Mobility: Redefining Transportation

37.1 Smart Public Transportation Systems

AI is transforming urban mobility by enabling smart public transportation systems. By analyzing ridership data and traffic patterns, AI can optimize routes and schedules, improving the efficiency of public transit and reducing congestion in urban areas.

37.2 Mobility as a Service (MaaS)

The concept of Mobility as a Service (MaaS) is gaining traction, with AI playing a central role. By integrating various transportation options into a single platform, AI can provide users with personalized travel recommendations, making it easier to navigate urban environments.

37.3 Sustainable Urban Mobility Solutions

AI can contribute to sustainable urban mobility solutions by promoting the use of electric vehicles, car-sharing services , and public transportation. By analyzing travel patterns and environmental data, AI can help cities develop strategies that reduce carbon emissions and promote greener transportation options. This shift not only benefits the environment but also enhances the quality of life for urban residents.

38. AI in Supply Chain Resilience: Building Robust Systems

38.1 Risk Management and Mitigation

AI is enhancing supply chain resilience by improving risk management and mitigation strategies. Machine learning algorithms can analyze data from various sources to identify potential disruptions, such as natural disasters or geopolitical events. By predicting these risks, organizations can develop contingency plans and adapt their supply chains accordingly.

38.2 Real-Time Supply Chain Visibility

AI technologies provide real-time visibility into supply chain operations, allowing companies to monitor inventory levels, shipment statuses, and supplier performance. This transparency enables organizations to respond quickly to changes and maintain operational efficiency, even in the face of unexpected challenges.

38.3 Collaboration and Communication

AI can facilitate collaboration and communication among supply chain partners. By analyzing data from multiple stakeholders, AI systems can identify opportunities for collaboration, streamline processes, and enhance overall supply chain performance. This collaborative approach fosters stronger relationships and improves resilience.

39. AI in Financial Forecasting: Enhancing Decision-Making

39.1 Predictive Analytics for Financial Planning

AI is transforming financial forecasting by providing predictive analytics that enhance decision-making. Machine learning algorithms can analyze historical financial data, market trends, and economic indicators to generate accurate forecasts. This capability enables organizations to make informed financial decisions and allocate resources effectively.

39.2 Risk Assessment in Investments

AI can improve risk assessment in investment strategies by analyzing vast amounts of data to identify potential risks and opportunities. By leveraging AI-driven insights, investors can make more informed decisions, optimizing their portfolios and minimizing exposure to market volatility.

39.3 Enhancing Financial Reporting

AI technologies can streamline financial reporting processes by automating data collection and analysis. This automation reduces the time and effort required for reporting, allowing finance teams to focus on strategic initiatives and improve overall financial performance.

40. AI in Smart Home Technology: Enhancing Daily Living

40.1 Home Automation

AI is revolutionizing smart home technology by enabling home automation systems that enhance daily living. From smart thermostats that learn user preferences to intelligent lighting systems that adjust based on occupancy, AI technologies create more comfortable and energy-efficient living environments.

40.2 Security and Surveillance

AI-powered security systems are enhancing home safety by providing real-time monitoring and alerts. These systems can analyze video feeds, detect unusual activity, and notify homeowners of potential threats, ensuring peace of mind.

40.3 Energy Management

AI can optimize energy management in smart homes by analyzing usage patterns and recommending energy-saving practices. By integrating with renewable energy sources, such as solar panels, AI systems can help homeowners reduce their carbon footprint and lower energy costs.

41. AI in Personal Finance: Empowering Financial Management

41.1 Budgeting and Expense Tracking

AI is transforming personal finance by providing tools for budgeting and expense tracking. AI-powered applications can analyze spending habits, categorize expenses, and offer personalized budgeting recommendations, helping individuals manage their finances more effectively.

41.2 Investment Management

AI technologies are enhancing investment management by providing personalized investment strategies based on individual financial goals and risk tolerance. By analyzing market trends and portfolio performance, AI can help users make informed investment decisions.

41.3 Financial Education

AI can support financial education by providing users with tailored resources and learning materials. By analyzing user behavior and knowledge gaps, AI systems can recommend educational content that empowers individuals to make better financial choices.

42. AI in Public Safety: Enhancing Community Security

42.1 Predictive Policing

AI is being utilized in predictive policing to enhance community safety. By analyzing crime data and patterns, AI systems can identify potential hotspots and allocate resources more effectively. This proactive approach enables law enforcement agencies to prevent crime and improve public safety.

42.2 Emergency Response Optimization

AI technologies can optimize emergency response efforts by analyzing data from various sources, including 911 calls and social media. By identifying trends and urgent needs, AI can help emergency services respond more efficiently and effectively during crises.

42.3 Community Engagement

AI can facilitate community engagement in public safety initiatives. By analyzing community feedback and concerns, AI systems can help law enforcement agencies develop strategies that address specific issues and foster trust between the police and the community.

43. AI in Cultural Heritage: Preserving History

43.1 Digital Preservation

AI is playing a crucial role in the digital preservation of cultural heritage. Machine learning algorithms can analyze and restore historical artifacts, documents, and artworks, ensuring that they are preserved for future generations. This technology enables museums and cultural institutions to maintain their collections and share them with a broader audience.

43.2 Enhancing Accessibility

AI technologies can enhance accessibility to cultural heritage by providing translation services and interactive experiences. By analyzing user preferences, AI can create personalized tours and educational content that engage diverse audiences, making cultural heritage more accessible to people from different backgrounds and languages.

43.3 Virtual Reality Experiences

AI is also being integrated into virtual reality (VR) experiences that allow users to explore historical sites and artifacts in immersive ways. By combining AI with VR, cultural institutions can create interactive environments where users can learn about history and culture through engaging simulations, enhancing their understanding and appreciation of heritage.

44. AI in Journalism: Transforming News Reporting

44.1 Automated News Generation

AI is revolutionizing journalism by enabling automated news generation. Machine learning algorithms can analyze data from various sources, including social media and public records, to produce news articles on topics such as sports, finance, and weather. This automation allows news organizations to deliver timely updates and cover a broader range of stories.

44.2 Fact-Checking and Verification

AI technologies are enhancing fact-checking processes in journalism. By analyzing claims and cross-referencing them with reliable sources, AI can assist journalists in verifying information before publication. This capability helps combat misinformation and ensures that news reporting maintains high standards of accuracy.

44.3 Personalized News Delivery

AI is also transforming how news is delivered to consumers. By analyzing user preferences and reading habits, AI algorithms can curate personalized news feeds that align with individual interests. This level of customization enhances user engagement and ensures that readers receive relevant content.

45. AI in Telecommunication: latest Innovations

45.1 Network Optimization

AI is playing a crucial role in optimizing telecommunications networks. Machine learning algorithms can analyze network performance data to identify areas for improvement, ensuring that users experience reliable connectivity and high-quality service.

45.2 Customer Support Automation

Telecommunications companies are leveraging AI to automate customer support processes. AI-powered chatbots can handle routine inquiries, troubleshoot issues, and provide account information, allowing human agents to focus on more complex customer needs. This automation enhances customer satisfaction by providing quick and efficient service.

45.3 Predictive Maintenance in Networks

AI can also play a crucial role in predictive maintenance for telecommunications networks. By analyzing data from network equipment, AI systems can predict potential failures and recommend maintenance before issues arise. This proactive approach minimizes downtime and ensures uninterrupted service for customers.

46. AI in Environmental Monitoring: Protecting Our Planet

46.1 Real-Time Environmental Data Analysis

AI is enhancing environmental monitoring by providing real-time data analysis. Machine learning algorithms can process data from sensors and satellites to monitor air and water quality, track wildlife populations, and assess the impact of climate change. This capability enables researchers and policymakers to make informed decisions to protect the environment.

46.2 Predictive Modeling for Conservation

AI can assist in conservation efforts by creating predictive models that forecast the impact of environmental changes on ecosystems. By analyzing historical data and current trends, AI can help identify vulnerable species and habitats, guiding conservation strategies to mitigate risks.

46.3 Community Engagement in Environmental Initiatives

AI technologies can facilitate community engagement in environmental initiatives by providing platforms for citizen science. By analyzing data collected by volunteers, AI can help communities monitor local environmental conditions and contribute to conservation efforts, fostering a sense of ownership and responsibility for the environment.

47. AI in Supply Chain Management: Enhancing Efficiency

47.1 Demand Forecasting

AI is transforming supply chain management by improving demand forecasting. Machine learning algorithms can analyze historical sales data, market trends, and external factors to predict future demand accurately. This capability enables organizations to optimize inventory levels and reduce costs.

47.2 Supplier Relationship Management

AI can enhance supplier relationship management by analyzing performance data and identifying potential risks. By monitoring supplier performance metrics, organizations can proactively address issues and strengthen partnerships, ensuring a more resilient supply chain.

47.3 Logistics Optimization

AI technologies are optimizing logistics operations by analyzing data related to transportation routes, delivery schedules, and inventory levels. This analysis enables organizations to streamline logistics processes, reduce costs, and improve overall supply chain efficiency.

48. AI in Smart Cities: Enhancing Urban Living

48.1 Intelligent Transportation Systems

AI is integral to the development of intelligent transportation systems in smart cities. By analyzing traffic data and user behavior, AI can optimize traffic flow, reduce congestion, and improve public transportation efficiency. This capability enhances urban mobility and contributes to a more sustainable transportation ecosystem.

48.2 Energy Management in Urban Areas

AI can optimize energy management in urban areas by analyzing consumption patterns and integrating renewable energy sources. Smart grids powered by AI can balance energy supply and demand, reducing waste and promoting sustainability in urban environments.

48.3 Public Safety and Emergency Response

AI technologies can enhance public safety in smart cities by analyzing data from surveillance systems and emergency services. Predictive analytics can help law enforcement agencies identify potential crime hotspots and allocate resources effectively, improving community safety.

III

The Challenges of AI

One of the biggest challenges of AI is developing systems that can truly understand and reason about the world. Another challenge is ensuring that AI systems are used ethically and responsibly.

- Ethical and responsible use of AI systems presents additional hurdles. Issues such as data privacy, accountability, and the potential for misuse of AI technologies are critical concerns. Ensuring that AI aligns with human values and moral principles is essential to mitigate risks associated with its deployment. This includes addressing the need for fairness, explainability, and robustness in AI systems, as well as fostering an environment where AI can be used to benefit society without infringing on individual rights or freedoms. AI faces a multitude of challenges that hinder its ability to understand and reason about the world effectively. Below are some of the key issues:

1. Understanding and Reasoning Challenges

- Data Dependency : AI systems rely heavily on large datasets for training. If these datasets contain biases or inaccuracies, the AI's understanding and reasoning will be flawed. This can lead to outcomes that reinforce existing stereotypes or inequalities.
- Contextual Understanding : AI often struggles with grasping context, which is crucial for reasoning. Unlike humans, AI lacks common sense and the ability to infer meaning from nuanced situations, making it difficult to apply knowledge appropriately in varied scenarios.
- Dynamic Environments : The world is constantly changing, and AI systems may not adapt quickly enough to new information or contexts. This rigidity can limit their effectiveness in real-world applications where adaptability is essential.

2. Ethical and Responsible Use

- Bias and Fairness : AI systems can perpetuate and even exacerbate biases present in their training data. Ensuring fairness in AI algorithms is a significant ethical concern, particularly in sensitive areas like hiring, lending, and law enforcement.
- Privacy Concerns : The collection and use of personal data by AI systems raise serious privacy issues. Users often lack awareness of how their data is being used, leading to potential violations of privacy rights.
- Accountability and Transparency : The 'black box' nature of many AI models makes it challenging to hold systems accountable for their decisions. Users and stakeholders need to understand how decisions are made to trust AI systems fully.
- Potential for Misuse : AI technologies can be exploited for malicious purposes, such as surveillance, misinformation, or even autonomous weapons. Establishing regulations and ethical guidelines is crucial to prevent misuse.

3. Addressing the Challenges

- Interdisciplinary Collaboration : Tackling these challenges requires collaboration among technologists, ethicists, policymakers, and the public. A multidisciplinary approach can help create comprehensive frameworks for ethical AI development.
- Regulatory Frameworks : Developing clear regulations that govern AI use is essential. These frameworks should address issues of accountability, transparency, and data privacy to ensure responsible AI deployment.
- Public Awareness and Education : Increasing public understanding of AI technologies and their implications can empower individuals to make informed choices about their data and the systems they interact with.

4. Future Directions

- Focus on Explainability : Enhancing the explainability of AI systems can help users understand how decisions are made, fostering trust and accountability.
- Ethical AI Design : Incorporating ethical considerations into the design and development of AI systems can help mitigate risks and ensure that AI technologies align with societal values.
- Continuous Monitoring and Evaluation : Ongoing assessment of AI systems is necessary to identify and address biases, ensuring that they remain fair and effective over time.
- In summary, while AI holds immense potential, addressing the challenges of understanding, reasoning, and ethical use is crucial for its successful integration into society. By focusing on these areas, we can harness the benefits of AI while minimizing its risks.

5. Societal Impacts

- Job Displacement : The rise of AI technologies poses a threat to traditional job markets, as automation can replace human labor in various sectors. This shift necessitates a reevaluation of workforce skills and the creation of new

job opportunities that leverage human creativity and emotional intelligence.
- Economic Inequality : As AI technologies advance, there is a risk that the benefits will be concentrated among a small group of companies and individuals, exacerbating economic disparities. Ensuring equitable access to AI resources and opportunities is vital to prevent widening the gap between different socioeconomic groups.
- Cultural Implications : The integration of AI into daily life can influence cultural norms and values. As AI systems become more prevalent, they may shape human interactions and societal expectations, leading to shifts in how we communicate, work, and relate to one another.

6. Technological Limitations

- Generalization : AI systems often excel in narrow tasks but struggle with generalizing knowledge across different domains. This limitation hinders their ability to perform well in diverse and unpredictable environments.
- Interpretability : Many advanced AI models, such as deep learning networks, are inherently complex and difficult to interpret. This lack of interpretability can hinder trust and acceptance among users, particularly in high-stakes applications like healthcare and finance.

7. Research and Development

- Advancements in AI Research : Ongoing research is essential to address the limitations of current AI systems. Innovations in areas such as natural language processing, computer vision, and reinforcement learning can enhance AI's understanding and reasoning capabilities.
- "Ethical AI Research": Prioritizing research that focuses on ethical considerations in AI development can lead to more responsible technologies. This includes exploring methods for bias detection and mitigation, as well as developing frameworks for ethical decision-making in AI systems.

"8. Global Cooperation"

- "International Standards": Establishing global standards for AI development and deployment can help ensure that ethical considerations are universally applied. International cooperation is crucial in addressing the cross-border implications of AI technologies.
- "Shared Knowledge": Collaborative efforts among countries, organizations, and researchers can facilitate the sharing of best practices and lessons learned in AI ethics and governance, promoting a more responsible approach to AI development worldwide.
- In conclusion, the challenges of AI are multifaceted, encompassing technical, ethical, societal, and economic dimensions. Addressing these challenges requires a concerted effort from various stakeholders, including researchers, policymakers, and the public. By fostering collaboration and prioritizing ethical considerations, we can navigate the complexities of AI and harness its potential for the greater good.

"9. Human-AI Collaboration"

- "Augmenting Human Capabilities": Rather than replacing humans, AI can be designed to augment human capabilities, enhancing productivity and creativity. This collaborative approach can lead to innovative solutions that leverage the strengths of both humans and machines.
- "Trust Building": Establishing trust between humans and AI systems is essential for effective collaboration. This involves creating AI that is reliable, transparent, and capable of explaining its reasoning to users, fostering a partnership that enhances decision-making processes.

"10. Environmental Considerations"

- "Energy Consumption": The training and operation of AI models can be resource-intensive, leading to significant energy consumption. Developing more efficient algorithms and hardware can help mitigate the environmental impact of AI technologies.

- "Sustainable AI Practices": Promoting sustainable practices in AI development, such as using renewable energy sources and optimizing resource usage, is crucial for minimizing the ecological footprint of AI systems.

"11. Legal and Regulatory Challenges"

- "Intellectual Property Issues": The rise of AI-generated content raises questions about intellectual property rights. Determining ownership and accountability for AI-created works is a complex legal challenge that needs to be addressed.
- "Liability and Accountability": As AI systems become more autonomous, establishing clear lines of liability for their actions is essential. This includes determining who is responsible when AI systems cause harm or make erroneous decisions.

"12. Psychological and Social Effects"

- "Impact on Mental Health": The pervasive use of AI in social media and communication can affect mental health, leading to issues such as addiction, anxiety, and social isolation. Understanding these effects is vital for developing healthier interactions with technology.
- "Shifts in Social Dynamics": AI can alter social dynamics by influencing how people interact and form relationships. The implications of these changes on community structures and social cohesion warrant careful examination.

"13. Education and Workforce Development"

- "Reskilling and Upskilling": As AI transforms job markets, there is a pressing need for reskilling and upskilling initiatives to prepare the workforce for new roles that emerge in an AI-driven economy. Educational institutions must adapt curricula to include AI literacy and related skills.
- "Lifelong Learning": Promoting a culture of lifelong learning is essential to help individuals continuously adapt to technological advancements and remain competitive in the job market.

"14. Ethical Frameworks and Guidelines"

- "Development of Ethical Guidelines": Establishing comprehensive ethical guidelines for AI development and deployment can help ensure that technologies are created with consideration for their societal impact. These guidelines should be informed by diverse perspectives and values.
- "Stakeholder Engagement": Involving various stakeholders, including marginalized communities, in the development of AI policies can lead to more equitable outcomes and ensure that diverse voices are heard in the decision-making process.

"15. Future Research Directions"

- "Interdisciplinary Approaches": Future research should embrace interdisciplinary approaches that combine insights from computer science, social sciences, and humanities to address the complex challenges posed by AI.
- "Long-term Implications": Investigating the long-term implications of AI on society, economy, and culture is crucial for understanding its potential trajectory and preparing for future developments.

- In summary, the challenges of AI are extensive and require a multifaceted approach to address effectively. By focusing on collaboration, sustainability, legal frameworks, and education, we can navigate the complexities of AI and work towards a future where technology serves humanity positively and ethically.

"16. Community Engagement and Public Discourse"

- "Encouraging Public Dialogue": Fostering open discussions about AI's implications can help demystify the technology and engage the public in meaningful conversations about its ethical use. This dialogue can lead to greater awareness and informed opinions on AI-related issues.
- "Participatory Design": Involving communities in the design and implementation of AI systems can ensure that these technologies reflect the needs and values of diverse populations. This participatory approach can enhance trust and acceptance of AI solutions.

"17. Cultural Sensitivity in AI Development"

- "Global Perspectives": AI systems should be developed with an understanding of cultural differences and sensitivities. This includes recognizing how AI may be perceived and utilized in various cultural contexts, ensuring that solutions are relevant and respectful.
- "Localization of AI Solutions": Tailoring AI applications to meet the specific needs of different communities can enhance their effectiveness and acceptance. This localization process should consider language, customs, and societal norms.

"18. The Role of Media and Communication"

- "Responsible Reporting": Media plays a crucial role in shaping public perception of AI. Responsible reporting on AI developments, including both benefits and risks, can help create a more informed public discourse.
- "Combating Misinformation": Addressing misinformation about AI technologies is essential to prevent fear and misunderstanding. Clear communication about AI capabilities and limitations can help build a more accurate public understanding.

"19. Technological Sovereignty"

- "National Strategies": Countries should develop national strategies for AI that prioritize local interests and capabilities. This includes investing in domestic AI research and development to ensure that nations can harness AI's potential independently.
- "Global Cooperation on AI Governance": International collaboration on AI governance can help address cross-border challenges and ensure that AI technologies are developed and used in ways that benefit humanity as a whole.

"20. The Future of Human-AI Interaction"

- "User -Centric Design": Designing AI systems with a focus on user experience can enhance usability and satisfaction. This involves understanding user needs and preferences to create intuitive interfaces and interactions.
- "Emotional Intelligence in AI": Developing AI systems that can recognize and respond to human emotions can improve interactions and foster more meaningful connections between humans and machines.

"21. The Impact of AI on Creativity"

- "AI as a Creative Partner": AI can serve as a tool for enhancing human creativity, providing new ways to generate ideas and solutions. This partnership can lead to innovative outcomes in fields such as art, music, and design.
- "Preserving Human Creativity": While AI can assist in creative processes, it is essential to ensure that human creativity remains at the forefront. Balancing AI's contributions with human input can lead to richer and more diverse creative expressions.

"22. Addressing the Digital Divide"

- "Equitable Access to AI Technologies": Ensuring that all communities have access to AI technologies is crucial for preventing disparities in benefits. This includes addressing infrastructure challenges and providing resources for underserved populations.
- "Bridging the Skills Gap": Initiatives aimed at bridging the skills gap in AI literacy can empower individuals from diverse backgrounds to participate in the AI-driven economy, fostering inclusivity and opportunity.

"23. The Role of Ethics in AI Education"

- "Integrating Ethics into AI Curricula": Educational programs focused on AI should incorporate ethical considerations, preparing future developers and users to navigate the moral implications of their work.
- "Promoting Ethical Leadership": Encouraging ethical leadership in AI development can help shape a culture of responsibility and accountability within organizations, ensuring that ethical considerations are prioritized in decision-making.

"24. The Importance of Feedback Loops"

- "Continuous Improvement": Establishing feedback loops between AI systems and users can facilitate ongoing learning and adaptation. This iterative process can help refine AI applications and enhance their effectiveness over time.
- "User Feedback Mechanisms": Implementing mechanisms for users to provide feedback on AI systems can help identify issues and areas for improvement, fostering a more responsive and user-centered approach to AI development.

"25. Challenges and opportunities"

- The challenges and opportunities presented by AI are vast and complex. By addressing these issues through collaboration, ethical considerations, and inclusive practices, we can work towards a future where AI technologies enhance human life while respecting individual rights and societal values. The journey ahead requires commitment from all stakeholders to ensure that AI serves as a force for good in society. "26. The Role of Government in AI Development"
- "Policy Frameworks": Governments play a crucial role in shaping the landscape of AI through the establishment of policy frameworks that promote innovation while ensuring ethical standards. These policies should encourage research and development while addressing potential risks associated with AI technologies.
- "Funding and Support": Providing funding and support for AI research initiatives can stimulate advancements in the field. Governments can invest in public-private partnerships to foster collaboration between academia and industry, driving innovation and application of AI solutions.

"32. The Role of Non-Governmental Organizations (NGOs)"

- "Advocacy for Ethical AI": NGOs can play a vital role in advocating for ethical AI practices and holding organizations accountable for their AI deployments. Their involvement can help ensure that marginalized voices are included in discussions about AI governance.
- "Community Engagement": NGOs can facilitate community engagement initiatives that educate the public about AI and its implications, fostering informed dialogue and participation in decision-making processes.

"33. The Importance of Interdisciplinary Research"

- "Bridging Knowledge Gaps": Interdisciplinary research that combines insights from various fields, such as computer science, sociology, and ethics, can lead to a more comprehensive understanding of AI's impact on society.
- "Innovative Solutions": Collaborative research efforts can drive innovative solutions to complex challenges, ensuring that AI technologies are developed with a holistic perspective that considers social, ethical, and technical dimensions.

"34. The Role of Industry in AI Ethics"

- "Corporate Responsibility": Companies developing AI technologies have a responsibility to prioritize ethical considerations in their practices. This includes implementing ethical guidelines, conducting impact assessments, and engaging with stakeholders to understand the societal implications of their products.
- "Transparency and Accountability": Industry leaders should promote transparency in AI development processes and be accountable for the outcomes of their technologies. This commitment can help build trust with users and the broader public.

"35. The Future of AI Governance"

- "Dynamic Regulatory Approaches": As AI technologies evolve, governance frameworks must also adapt to address emerging challenges. Dynamic regulatory approaches that can respond to rapid technological advancements are essential for effective oversight.
- "Global Collaboration on Governance": International cooperation is crucial for establishing governance frameworks that address the global nature of AI technologies. Collaborative efforts can help create standards that promote ethical AI development worldwide.

IV

The future of AI

The future of AI is poised to significantly transform various sectors, including healthcare, banking, and transportation, potentially increasing global GDP by 14% by 2030. While AI may displace some jobs, it is also expected to create new roles and enhance productivity, necessitating a focus on ethical use and equitable access to technology. AI's evolution is marked by rapid advancements, with the potential to revolutionize industries and improve quality of life. As AI technologies become more integrated into daily operations, their impact will be profound and multifaceted.

"1. Healthcare Innovations"

- AI is set to enhance diagnostic accuracy, enabling early detection of diseases and personalized treatment plans.
- Predictive analytics can improve patient outcomes by anticipating health issues before they arise.
- Telemedicine powered by AI can increase access to healthcare, especially in underserved areas, allowing for remote consultations and monitoring.

"2. Economic Transformation"

- The integration of AI into business processes can lead to significant productivity gains, streamlining operations and reducing costs.
- AI-driven automation may reshape job markets, requiring workers to adapt to new roles that emphasize creativity and emotional intelligence.
- The financial sector will see AI algorithms optimizing trading strategies and risk management, potentially disrupting traditional practices.

"3. Transportation Advancements"

- Autonomous vehicles are becoming a reality, promising to reduce traffic accidents and improve efficiency in logistics and public transport.
- AI can enhance traffic management systems, optimizing routes and reducing congestion in urban areas.
- Smart transportation solutions will integrate AI with IoT devices, providing real-time data for better decision-making.

"4. Ethical Considerations"

- As AI systems become more prevalent, ensuring ethical use is paramount. This includes addressing biases in algorithms and promoting fairness in decision-making processes.

- Privacy concerns will need to be managed, particularly regarding data collection and usage in AI applications.
- Establishing regulatory frameworks will be essential to guide the responsible development and deployment of AI technologies.

"5. Education and Workforce Development"

- AI can personalize learning experiences, adapting educational content to meet individual student needs and improving engagement.
- The workforce will require reskilling and upskilling initiatives to prepare for the changing job landscape, emphasizing lifelong learning.
- Educational institutions must incorporate AI literacy into curricula to equip future generations with the necessary skills.

"6. Environmental Impact"

- AI can contribute to sustainability efforts by optimizing resource use and improving energy efficiency in various sectors.
- Predictive models powered by AI can enhance environmental monitoring and inform policy decisions related to climate change.
- Developing sustainable AI practices will be crucial to minimize the ecological footprint of AI technologies.

"7. Global Cooperation and Governance"

- International collaboration will be necessary to establish global standards for AI development and deployment, ensuring ethical considerations are universally applied.
- Governments and organizations must work together to address the cross-border implications of AI technologies, fostering a responsible approach to AI governance.
- Engaging diverse stakeholders in discussions about AI policies can lead to more equitable outcomes and ensure that marginalized voices are heard.

"8. Future Research Directions"

- o Ongoing research in AI will focus on enhancing understanding and reasoning capabilities, addressing current limitations in AI systems.
- o Ethical AI research will prioritize bias detection and mitigation, ensuring that technologies align with societal values.
- o Interdisciplinary approaches will be essential to tackle the complex challenges posed by AI, combining insights from various fields.

"9. Human-AI Collaboration"

- o The future of AI will likely involve increased collaboration between humans and machines, where AI augments human capabilities rather than replacing them.
- o Building trust between humans and AI systems will be crucial for effective collaboration, requiring transparency and explainability in AI decision-making.
- o Emotional intelligence in AI can improve interactions, fostering meaningful connections between humans and machines.

"10. Conclusion"

- ➢ The future of AI holds immense potential to reshape industries, enhance quality of life, and address global challenges. However, realizing this potential requires a commitment to ethical practices, equitable access, and ongoing collaboration among stakeholders. By navigating the complexities of AI responsibly, society can harness its benefits while minimizing risks, paving the way for a brighter future. The future of AI is not only about technological advancements but also about the societal implications that come with them. As AI continues to evolve, it will be essential to consider how these changes affect various aspects of life, including social structures, economic systems, and individual experiences.

"11. Social Dynamics"

- o AI has the potential to alter social interactions, influencing how people communicate and form relationships.
- o The integration of AI in social media platforms can shape public discourse, impacting opinions and behaviors on a large scale.
- o Understanding the psychological effects of AI on social dynamics will be crucial for fostering healthy interactions in an increasingly digital world.

"12. Cultural Shifts"

- o The adoption of AI technologies may lead to cultural shifts, as societies adapt to new ways of living and working.
- o AI can influence creative industries, changing how art, music, and literature are produced and consumed.
- o Recognizing and respecting cultural differences in AI development will be vital to ensure that technologies are inclusive and relevant to diverse populations.

"13. Security and Safety"

- o As AI systems become more integrated into critical infrastructure, ensuring their security against cyber threats will be paramount.
- o Developing robust safety protocols for autonomous systems, such as self-driving cars and drones, will be essential to prevent accidents and ensure public trust.
- o Addressing the ethical implications of AI in security applications, such as surveillance and law enforcement, will require careful consideration of privacy rights and civil liberties.

"14. AI in Governance"

o Governments may leverage AI to improve public services, enhance decision-making processes, and increase efficiency in administration.

o However, the use of AI in governance raises questions about accountability, transparency, and the potential for bias in automated decision-making.

o Engaging citizens in discussions about the role of AI in governance can help build trust and ensure that technologies serve the public interest.

"15. The Role of Startups and Innovation"

o Startups will play a crucial role in driving innovation in the AI space, often pushing the boundaries of what is possible.

o Encouraging a vibrant startup ecosystem can lead to breakthroughs that address pressing societal challenges, from healthcare to climate change.

o Supporting entrepreneurship in AI will require access to funding, mentorship, and resources to help new ventures succeed.

"16. The Importance of Ethics in AI Development"

o Ethical considerations must be at the forefront of AI development, guiding the design and implementation of technologies.

o Establishing ethical review boards and frameworks can help organizations navigate the complexities of AI ethics and ensure responsible practices.

o Promoting a culture of ethical awareness within organizations will be essential for fostering accountability and trust in AI systems.

"17. The Impact of AI on Global Inequality"

o The benefits of AI may not be evenly distributed, potentially exacerbating existing inequalities between nations and communities.

o Ensuring equitable access to AI technologies and resources will be crucial for preventing a widening gap between those who can leverage AI and those who cannot.

o International cooperation and support for developing countries in AI adoption can help create a more balanced global landscape.

"18. The Future of AI Research"

o Research in AI will continue to explore new frontiers, including advancements in machine learning, natural language processing, and robotics.
o Collaborative research efforts that involve academia, industry, and government can drive innovation and address complex challenges.
o Fostering a culture of curiosity and exploration in AI research will be essential for unlocking its full potential.

"19. The Role of Public Policy"

o Policymakers will need to adapt regulations to keep pace with the rapid evolution of AI technologies, ensuring that they are safe and beneficial for society.
o Public policy should promote innovation while safeguarding ethical standards and protecting individual rights.
o Engaging with experts and stakeholders in the development of AI policies can lead to more informed and effective regulations.

"20. Conclusion"

➢ The future of AI is a landscape filled with opportunities and challenges. As society navigates this evolving terrain, it will be essential to prioritize ethical considerations, foster collaboration, and ensure that the benefits of AI are accessible to all. By embracing a holistic approach to AI development and deployment, we can work towards a future where technology enhances human life and addresses the pressing issues of our time. The future of AI is not just about technological advancements; it encompasses a broader vision of how these technologies will shape our lives, societies, and the world at large. As AI continues to evolve, its integration into various sectors will lead to profound changes that require careful consideration and proactive measures.

"21. Workforce Transformation"

- o The nature of work will change significantly, with AI taking over repetitive tasks and allowing humans to focus on more complex and creative endeavors.
- o New job categories will emerge, necessitating a shift in skills and training programs to prepare the workforce for an AI-driven economy.
- o Collaboration between humans and AI will become the norm, enhancing productivity and innovation across industries.

"22. AI in Creative Industries"

- o AI's role in creative fields, such as art, music, and writing, will expand, leading to new forms of expression and collaboration.
- o While AI can generate content, the unique human touch will remain essential, fostering a partnership that enhances creativity rather than replacing it.
- o The ethical implications of AI-generated content, including issues of authorship and originality, will need to be addressed.

"23. AI and Personalization"

- o AI will enable highly personalized experiences in various domains, from marketing to healthcare, tailoring services to individual preferences and needs.
- o This personalization can enhance user satisfaction and engagement, but it also raises concerns about privacy and data security.
- o Striking a balance between personalization and ethical data use will be crucial for maintaining trust with users.

"24. AI in Public Safety"

- o AI technologies will play a significant role in enhancing public safety through predictive policing, emergency response optimization, and disaster management.
- o However, the use of AI in law enforcement raises ethical questions about surveillance, bias, and civil liberties that must be carefully navigated.
- o Community engagement and transparency in the deployment of AI for public safety will be essential to build trust and accountability.

"25. The Role of AI in Climate Action"

- o AI can contribute to climate change mitigation by optimizing energy consumption, improving resource management, and enhancing climate modeling.
- o Innovative AI solutions can support sustainable practices across industries, helping to reduce carbon footprints and promote environmental stewardship.
- o Collaboration between governments, businesses, and researchers will be vital to harness AI's potential for climate action effectively.

"26. AI and Global Health"

- o The application of AI in global health can improve disease surveillance, outbreak prediction, and resource allocation, particularly in low-resource settings.
- o AI-driven solutions can enhance access to healthcare services, especially in remote areas, by facilitating telemedicine and remote diagnostics.
- o Addressing ethical considerations, such as data privacy and equity in healthcare access, will be crucial for successful implementation.

"27. The Future of AI Ethics"

- o As AI technologies become more integrated into society, the need for robust ethical frameworks will grow.

- Organizations must prioritize ethical considerations in AI development, ensuring that technologies are designed with fairness, accountability, and transparency in mind.
- Ongoing dialogue among stakeholders, including ethicists, technologists, and the public, will be essential to navigate the ethical landscape of AI.

"28. AI and Human Rights"

- The intersection of AI and human rights will become increasingly important, as technologies can both support and undermine individual rights.
- Ensuring that AI systems respect human rights, including privacy, freedom of expression, and non-discrimination, will be a critical challenge.
- Advocacy and policy efforts will be necessary to protect human rights in the context of AI deployment and use.

"29. The Role of Education in AI Literacy"

- Education systems must adapt to equip students with the skills needed to thrive in an AI-driven world, emphasizing critical thinking, creativity, and digital literacy.
- AI literacy programs can empower individuals to understand and engage with AI technologies, fostering informed citizens who can navigate the complexities of the digital age.
- Lifelong learning initiatives will be essential to ensure that the workforce remains adaptable and competitive in the face of rapid technological change.

"30. Conclusion"

- The future of AI presents a landscape rich with possibilities and challenges. As society embraces these technologies, it is imperative to prioritize ethical considerations, foster collaboration, and ensure that the benefits of AI are accessible to all. By taking a proactive approach to AI development and deployment, we can work towards a future where technology enhances human life, addresses pressing global issues, and promotes a more equitable and sustainable world. The journey ahead will require commitment, innovation, and a shared vision for a better future. "31. The Role of AI in Enhancing Accessibility"

- o AI technologies can significantly improve accessibility for individuals with disabilities, providing tools that facilitate communication, mobility, and daily activities.
- o Innovations such as speech recognition, text-to-speech, and computer vision can empower users to interact with their environments more effectively.
- o Ensuring that AI solutions are designed with inclusivity in mind will be essential to maximize their benefits for all users.

"32. AI and the Future of Retail"

- o The retail sector will undergo transformation through AI-driven personalization, inventory management, and customer service enhancements.
- o AI can analyze consumer behavior to tailor marketing strategies and improve the shopping experience, leading to increased customer satisfaction.
- o However, retailers must balance automation with the human touch to maintain meaningful customer relationships.

"33. AI in Financial Services"

- o AI will revolutionize financial services by enhancing fraud detection, risk assessment, and customer service through chatbots and virtual assistants.
- o Predictive analytics can help financial institutions make informed decisions and offer personalized financial advice to clients.
- o Regulatory compliance will be a critical consideration as AI systems are integrated into financial operations, necessitating transparency and accountability.

"34. The Impact of AI on Supply Chain Management"

- AI can optimize supply chain operations by improving demand forecasting, inventory management, and logistics planning.
- Enhanced data analytics will enable companies to respond more effectively to market changes and consumer demands.
- Collaboration between AI systems and human decision-makers will be crucial for achieving efficiency and resilience in supply chains.

"35. AI and Cybersecurity"

- As cyber threats evolve, AI will play a vital role in enhancing cybersecurity measures, enabling organizations to detect and respond to threats in real-time.
- Machine learning algorithms can analyze patterns and anomalies in network traffic, identifying potential vulnerabilities before they are exploited.
- However, the use of AI in cybersecurity also raises concerns about the potential for misuse and the need for ethical considerations in its deployment.

"36. The Role of AI in Scientific Research"

- AI can accelerate scientific discovery by analyzing vast datasets, identifying patterns, and generating hypotheses.
- In fields such as genomics and drug discovery, AI-driven insights can lead to breakthroughs that were previously unattainable.
- Collaboration between AI researchers and domain experts will be essential to ensure that AI applications are relevant and effective in advancing scientific knowledge.

"37. AI and the Future of Journalism"

- AI technologies can assist journalists in data analysis, fact-checking, and content generation, enhancing the efficiency of news production.

- However, the rise of AI-generated content raises ethical questions about authenticity, bias, and the role of human journalists in maintaining journalistic integrity.
- Media organizations must navigate these challenges to ensure that AI serves as a tool for enhancing, rather than undermining, the quality of journalism.

"38. The Role of AI in Disaster Response"

- AI can improve disaster response efforts by analyzing data from various sources to predict and mitigate the impact of natural disasters.
- Machine learning algorithms can assist in resource allocation, logistics planning, and real-time decision-making during emergencies.
- Collaboration between AI systems and emergency responders will be crucial for effective disaster management and recovery.

"39. AI and the Future of Gaming"

- The gaming industry will continue to leverage AI to create more immersive and dynamic experiences for players, enhancing gameplay and storytelling.
- AI can adapt game environments and challenges based on player behavior, providing personalized experiences that keep players engaged.
- Ethical considerations, such as the impact of AI on player behavior and addiction, will need to be addressed as gaming technologies evolve.

"40. Conclusion"

➢ The future of AI is a multifaceted landscape that promises to reshape various aspects of life, from healthcare to entertainment. As society embraces these advancements, it is crucial to prioritize ethical considerations, foster collaboration, and ensure that the benefits of AI are accessible to all. By navigating the complexities of AI responsibly, we can harness its potential to create a better future for individuals and communities worldwide. The journey ahead will require innovation, adaptability, and a commitment to inclusivity and equity in the development and deployment of AI technologies.

V

How to Use AI as a Tool

➤ Artificial Intelligence (AI) has rapidly evolved over the past few decades, transforming the way individuals and businesses operate. From automating mundane tasks to providing insights through data analysis, AI has become an indispensable tool in various sectors. However, to harness its full potential, it is crucial to understand how to use AI effectively, recognizing both its capabilities and limitations. This guide will explore the effective use of AI, focusing on understanding its limitations, leveraging its strengths, and considering the ethical implications of its application.

➢ Understanding the Limitations of AI

1. Imperfection and Error

AI systems are not infallible. They are designed to learn from data, and their performance is heavily dependent on the quality and quantity of that data. Here are some key points to consider:

➢ Data Quality

AI models trained on biased or incomplete data can produce skewed results. For instance, facial recognition systems have been shown to misidentify individuals from certain demographic groups due to a lack of diverse training data. This can lead to significant real-world consequences, such as wrongful arrests or discrimination in hiring practices.

➢ Contextual Understanding

AI lacks true understanding and reasoning capabilities. It can process information and identify patterns but does not comprehend context in the way humans do. This can lead to errors in judgment, especially in nuanced situations. For example, an AI system might misinterpret sarcasm in a text, leading to inappropriate responses in customer service applications.

➢ Overfitting and Generalization

AI models can become too tailored to their training data, a phenomenon known as overfitting. This means they may perform well on familiar data but poorly on new, unseen data. For instance, a model trained on a specific dataset of images may fail to recognize objects in images that differ significantly from the training set.

2. Lack of Emotional Intelligence

AI systems do not possess emotional intelligence. They cannot empathize, understand human emotions, or navigate complex social interactions. This limitation is particularly significant in fields such as healthcare, customer service, and education, where human interaction is crucial. For example, while an AI can provide medical information, it cannot offer the compassion and understanding that a human doctor can provide during a difficult diagnosis.

3. Dependence on Human Oversight

Despite advancements in AI, human oversight remains essential. AI can assist in decision-making but should not replace human judgment entirely. For example, in legal settings, AI can analyze case law and suggest outcomes, but a qualified attorney must interpret the results and make final decisions. This ensures that ethical considerations and human values are taken into account.

• Using AI for Tasks It Excels At

1. Pattern Recognition

AI is particularly adept at tasks involving pattern recognition. This includes:

➢ **Image Classification**

AI can analyze images and classify them based on learned features. Applications range from medical imaging (e.g., detecting tumors) to security (e.g., facial recognition). In healthcare, AI algorithms can assist radiologists by highlighting areas of concern in medical scans, improving diagnostic accuracy.

➢ **Natural Language Processing (NLP)**

AI can process and analyze human language, enabling applications such as chatbots, sentiment analysis, and language translation. Businesses can use NLP to enhance customer interactions and streamline communication. For instance, AI-driven chatbots can handle customer inquiries 24/7, providing instant responses and freeing human agents to focus on more complex issues.

2. Data Analysis and Insights

AI can analyze vast amounts of data quickly and efficiently, uncovering insights that would be difficult for humans to identify. This capability is invaluable in various fields:

> ➤ **Business Intelligence**

AI can analyze sales data, customer behavior, and market trends, helping businesses make informed decisions. For example, predictive analytics can forecast sales trends, allowing companies to optimize inventory and marketing strategies.

> ➤ **Healthcare**

AI can analyze patient data to identify trends, predict outcomes, and assist in diagnosis, ultimately improving patient care. For instance, AI algorithms can predict patient deterioration based on real-time monitoring data, enabling timely interventions.

3. Automation of Repetitive Tasks

AI can automate repetitive and mundane tasks, freeing up human resources for more complex and creative work. Examples include:

> ➤ **Administrative Tasks**

AI can handle scheduling, data entry, and document management, increasing efficiency in office environments. For example, AI-powered tools can automatically sort and prioritize emails, allowing employees to focus on more critical tasks.

> ➤ **Manufacturing**

AI-powered robots can perform repetitive tasks on assembly lines, improving productivity and reducing human error. These robots can work alongside human workers, enhancing overall efficiency and safety in manufacturing environments.

> ➤ **Ethical Implications of Using AI**

1. Bias and Fairness

One of the most pressing ethical concerns surrounding AI is bias. AI systems can perpetuate and even exacerbate existing biases present in training data. To mitigate this risk:

> ➢ **Diverse Data Sets**

Ensure that training data is diverse and representative of the population to avoid biased outcomes. This includes actively seeking out underrepresented groups in data collection efforts.

> ➢ **Regular Audits**

Conduct regular audits of AI systems to identify and address biases in decision-making processes. This can involve testing AI outputs against diverse scenarios to ensure fairness and equity in results.

2. Privacy Concerns

AI often relies on large datasets, which can include sensitive personal information. This raises significant privacy concerns:

> ➢ **Data Protection**

Implement robust data protection measures to safeguard personal information and comply with regulations such as GDPR. Organizations should adopt encryption, anonymization, and secure data storage practices to protect user data.

> ➢ **Transparency**

Be transparent about how data is collected, used, and stored. Users should have the right to know how their data is being utilized, including the purposes for which it is processed and the duration of data retention.

3. Accountability and Responsibility

As AI systems become more autonomous, questions of accountability arise. If an AI system makes a mistake, who is responsible? To address this issue:

➢ Clear Guidelines

Establish clear guidelines for accountability in AI decision-making processes. Organizations should define roles and responsibilities for AI oversight, ensuring that there is a clear chain of accountability.

➢ Human Oversight

Maintain human oversight in critical areas, ensuring that humans remain responsible for final decisions. This is particularly important in high-stakes environments such as healthcare and criminal justice, where AI decisions can have significant consequences.

4. Job Displacement

The automation of tasks through AI can lead to job displacement in certain sectors. While AI can create new job opportunities, it is essential to consider the impact on the workforce:

➢ Reskilling and Upskilling

Invest in reskilling and upskilling programs to help workers transition to new roles in an AI-driven economy. This can involve training programs that focus on digital literacy, critical thinking, and advanced technical skills.

➢ Job Creation

While some jobs may be lost, AI can also create new roles that did not exist before, particularly in areas such as AI development, maintenance, and oversight. Encouraging innovation and entrepreneurship can help mitigate the effects of job displacement.

➢ Best Practices for Implementing AI

1. Start Small and Scale Gradually

When integrating AI into business processes, it is advisable to start with small pilot projects. This allows organizations to test AI applications in a controlled environment, assess their effectiveness, and make necessary adjustments before scaling up.

2. Foster a Culture of Collaboration

Encouraging collaboration between AI specialists and domain experts is crucial for successful AI implementation. Domain experts can provide valuable insights into the specific challenges and requirements of their fields, ensuring that AI solutions are tailored to meet real-world needs.

3. Continuous Learning and Adaptation

AI technology is constantly evolving, and organizations must be willing to adapt. This involves staying informed about the latest advancements in AI, regularly updating systems, and being open to feedback from users to improve AI applications continuously.

4. Engage Stakeholders

Involve stakeholders from various levels of the organization in the AI implementation process. This includes not only technical teams but also end-users who will interact with AI systems. Their input can help identify potential challenges and ensure that the AI solutions meet user needs.

> ### Further Exploration of AI as a Tool

1. Enhancing Creativity with AI

AI can also play a significant role in enhancing creativity across various fields. By providing tools that assist in the creative process, AI can help individuals and teams generate new ideas and solutions. Here are some ways AI can enhance creativity:

> ### Content Generation

AI can assist in generating written content, music, and art. For instance, AI algorithms can analyze existing works to create new compositions or suggest improvements to drafts, allowing creators to explore new avenues of expression.

> ➢ **Design Assistance**

In fields like graphic design and architecture, AI can help generate design options based on user preferences and constraints, enabling designers to focus on refining and innovating rather than starting from scratch.

2. AI in Education

The integration of AI in education has the potential to personalize learning experiences and improve educational outcomes. Here are some applications of AI in education:

> ➢ **Personalized Learning**

AI can analyze student performance data to tailor educational content to individual learning styles and paces, ensuring that each student receives the support they need to succeed.

> ➢ **Intelligent Tutoring Systems**

AI-powered tutoring systems can provide real-time feedback and assistance to students, helping them grasp complex concepts and improve their skills outside of traditional classroom settings.

3. AI in Healthcare

AI's impact on healthcare is profound, with applications that can enhance patient care and streamline operations. Some key areas include:

> ➢ **Predictive Analytics**

AI can analyze patient data to predict health outcomes, enabling proactive interventions that can improve patient health and reduce hospital readmissions.

> ➢ **Drug Discovery**

AI can accelerate the drug discovery process by analyzing vast datasets to identify potential drug candidates, significantly reducing the time and cost associated with bringing new medications to market.

4. AI in Customer Service

AI is transforming customer service by providing efficient and effective solutions. Here are some ways AI is being utilized:

> **Chatbots and Virtual Assistants**

AI-powered chatbots can handle customer inquiries 24/7, providing instant responses and freeing human agents to focus on more complex issues. These chatbots can learn from interactions, improving their responses over time and enhancing customer satisfaction.

> **Sentiment Analysis**

AI can analyze customer feedback and interactions to gauge sentiment, helping businesses understand customer satisfaction and identify areas for improvement. By processing large volumes of data, AI can uncover trends and insights that inform product development and marketing strategies.

5. Future Trends in AI

As AI technology continues to evolve, several trends are emerging that will shape its future applications:

> **Explainable AI (XAI)**

There is a growing demand for AI systems that can explain their decision-making processes. This transparency is crucial for building trust and ensuring accountability in AI applications. Organizations are increasingly focusing on developing models that provide clear rationales for their outputs, making it easier for users to understand and trust AI decisions.

> **AI and IoT Integration**

The integration of AI with the Internet of Things (IoT) will enable smarter devices that can learn from their environments and make autonomous decisions, enhancing efficiency and user experience. For example, smart home devices can optimize energy usage based on user habits, while industrial IoT applications can predict equipment failures before they occur.

> **AI for Sustainability**

AI can play a vital role in addressing environmental challenges by optimizing resource use, reducing waste, and improving energy efficiency across various industries. For instance, AI algorithms can analyze energy consumption patterns in buildings to suggest improvements, leading to significant reductions in carbon footprints.

6. Building an AI-Ready Workforce

To fully leverage the potential of AI, organizations must invest in building an AI-ready workforce. This involves:

> **Training Programs**

Implementing training programs that focus on AI literacy, data analysis, and machine learning concepts to equip employees with the necessary skills to work alongside AI technologies. This can include workshops, online courses, and hands-on projects that foster practical understanding.

> **Cross-Disciplinary Collaboration**

Encouraging collaboration between technical teams and domain experts to foster innovation and ensure that AI solutions are relevant and effective. By bringing together diverse perspectives, organizations can create more comprehensive and impactful AI applications.

7. Conclusion

> AI is a powerful tool that can enhance productivity, creativity, and decision-making across various sectors. By understanding its limitations, leveraging its strengths, and addressing ethical considerations, individuals and organizations can effectively integrate AI into their operations. As we continue to explore the potential of AI, it is essential to remain committed to responsible practices that prioritize human well-being and societal benefits. The future of AI holds immense promise, and with thoughtful implementation, it can serve as a catalyst for positive change in our world.

8. Recommendations for Future Research

To further enhance the understanding and application of AI as a tool, future research should focus on:

> **Longitudinal Studies**

Conducting longitudinal studies to assess the long-term impacts of AI implementation on various sectors, including workforce dynamics, productivity, and ethical considerations.

> **Interdisciplinary Approaches**

Encouraging interdisciplinary research that combines insights from AI, ethics, sociology, and economics to develop holistic frameworks for AI deployment.

> **Policy Development**

Investigating the role of policy in shaping AI development and deployment, ensuring that regulations keep pace with technological advancements while promoting innovation and protecting public interests.

By addressing these areas, stakeholders can better navigate the complexities of AI and maximize its benefits while minimizing potential risks.

- **Using AI as a tool can be beneficial for students, job workers, and businessmen in various ways. Here are some examples:**

"For Students:"

1. "Personalized learning": AI can help students learn at their own pace by providing personalized learning experiences. AI-powered adaptive learning systems can adjust the difficulty level of course materials based on a student's performance, helping them to learn more effectively.

2. "Automated grading": AI can help teachers with grading, freeing up time for more important tasks. AI-powered grading systems can also provide instant feedback to students, helping them to identify areas where they need to improve.

3. "Research assistance": AI can help students with research by providing them with relevant information and sources. AI-powered research tools can also help students to organize their research and provide citations.

4. "Language learning": AI-powered language learning tools can help students to learn new languages by providing them with interactive lessons and exercises.

"For Job Workers:"

1. "Task automation": AI can help job workers by automating repetitive and mundane tasks, freeing up time for more important tasks. AI-powered tools can also help workers to prioritize tasks and manage their time more effectively.

2. "Data analysis": AI can help job workers to analyze large datasets and provide insights that can inform business decisions. AI-powered data analysis tools can also help workers to identify trends and patterns in data.

3. "Customer service": AI-powered chatbots can help job workers to provide better customer service by providing instant responses to customer inquiries.

4. "Skill development": AI-powered training tools can help job workers to develop new skills and improve their performance.

"For Businessmen:"

1. "Market research": AI can help businessmen to conduct market research by analyzing large datasets and providing insights that can inform business decisions. AI-powered market research tools can also help businessmen to identify trends and patterns in data.

2. "Predictive analytics": AI-powered predictive analytics tools can help businessmen to predict future trends and patterns in data, helping them to make informed business decisions.

3. "Customer segmentation": AI can help businessmen to segment their customers based on their behavior and preferences, helping them to provide more targeted marketing and sales efforts.

4. "Supply chain optimization": AI-powered supply chain optimization tools can help businessmen to optimize their supply chain operations, reducing costs and improving efficiency.

"Common benefits for all:"

1. "Increased productivity": AI can help students, job workers, and businessmen to increase their productivity by automating repetitive and mundane tasks.

2. "Improved decision-making": AI can help students, job workers, and businessmen to make more informed decisions by providing them with data-driven insights.

3. "Enhanced customer experience": AI can help students, job workers, and businessmen to provide better customer service by providing instant responses to customer inquiries.

4. "Competitive advantage": AI can help students, job workers, and businessmen to gain a competitive advantage by providing them with unique insights and capabilities.

Overall, AI can be a powerful tool for students, job workers, and businessmen, helping them to increase their productivity, improve their decision-making, and gain a competitive advantage. "Using AI as a Tool for Students, Job Workers, and Businessmen"

- **AI technology has become an essential resource across various sectors, providing unique advantages to students, job workers, and businessmen. Here's how each group can effectively utilize AI:**

"For Students:"

1. "Study Assistance":
    a. AI-powered platforms can offer personalized study plans based on individual learning styles and progress.
    b. Tools like Quizlet and Anki use AI to create adaptive flashcards that help reinforce learning.
2. "Time Management":
    a. AI scheduling tools can help students manage their time effectively by organizing study sessions around classes and work commitments.
    b. Applications like Notion and Trello can integrate AI features to prioritize tasks and deadlines.
3. "Writing Support":
    a. AI writing assistants like Grammarly and Hemingway can help students improve their writing by providing real-time feedback on grammar, style, and clarity.
    b. AI can also assist in generating outlines and brainstorming ideas for essays and research papers.
4. "Collaboration Tools":
    a. AI-driven collaboration platforms can facilitate group projects by organizing tasks, setting deadlines, and tracking progress.
    b. Tools like Google Docs and Microsoft Teams use AI to enhance communication and document sharing among peers.

"For Job Workers:"

1. "Enhanced Productivity":
    a. AI tools can automate routine tasks such as data entry, scheduling, and email management, allowing workers to focus on more strategic activities.
    b. Applications like Zapier can connect different software tools to automate workflows.

2. "Data-Driven Insights":
   a. AI analytics tools can help workers analyze performance metrics and customer feedback, leading to informed decision-making.
   b. Platforms like Tableau and Power BI utilize AI to visualize data trends and insights effectively.
3. "Skill Development":
   a. AI-powered learning platforms can provide personalized training programs tailored to individual career goals and skill gaps.
   b. Tools like LinkedIn Learning and Coursera offer courses that adapt to the learner's pace and preferences.
4. "Remote Work Facilitation":
   a. AI can enhance remote work experiences by optimizing communication and collaboration through virtual assistants and chatbots.
   b. Tools like Slack and Microsoft Teams leverage AI to streamline team interactions and project management.

"For Businessmen:"

1. "Market Analysis":
   a. AI can analyze market trends and consumer behavior, providing insights that inform product development and marketing strategies.
   b. Tools like Google Analytics and SEMrush use AI to track user engagement and optimize marketing campaigns.
2. "Customer Relationship Management (CRM)":
   a. AI-driven CRM systems can help businesses manage customer interactions, predict customer needs, and personalize marketing efforts.
   b. Platforms like Salesforce and HubSpot utilize AI to enhance customer engagement and retention.
3. "Operational Efficiency":
   a. AI can optimize supply chain management by predicting demand, managing inventory, and reducing operational costs.
   b. Tools like IBM Watson Supply Chain use AI to enhance logistics and inventory management.
4. "Financial Forecasting":
   a. AI can assist in financial planning and forecasting by analyzing historical data and predicting future trends.

b. Tools like QuickBooks and Xero leverage AI to provide insights into cash flow and financial health.

"Common Benefits Across All Groups:"

a. "Increased Efficiency":
   i. AI can streamline processes, reducing the time spent on repetitive tasks and allowing for more focus on critical thinking and creativity.
b. "Improved Accuracy":
   i. AI systems can minimize human error in data analysis and decision-making, leading to more reliable outcomes.
c. "Enhanced Learning and Development":
   i. AI can provide tailored learning experiences, helping individuals acquire new skills and knowledge relevant to their fields.
d. "Competitive Edge":
   i. By leveraging AI, students, job workers, and businessmen can stay ahead of the curve, adapting to changes in their respective environments more swiftly.

In conclusion, AI serves as a versatile tool that can significantly enhance the capabilities of students, job workers, and businessmen alike. By understanding and utilizing AI effectively, each group can improve productivity, decision-making, and overall success in their endeavours. "Using AI as a Tool for Students, Job Workers, and Businessmen"

AI technology has become an essential resource across various sectors, providing unique advantages to students, job workers, and businessmen.

- **AI is transforming graphic design, editing, and writing by automating repetitive tasks, enhancing creativity, and streamlining workflows. It allows designers and writers to focus on higher-level creative processes while tools generate layouts, suggest edits, and provide real-time feedback, significantly improving efficiency and productivity.**

AI in Graphic Design.

- o "Automated Design Generation": AI tools can create unique designs based on user inputs, allowing designers to generate multiple variations quickly. This speeds up the ideation process and provides fresh inspiration.
- o "Layout Suggestions": AI can analyze design principles and suggest optimal layouts, saving time on trial and error. Tools like Adobe Firefly and Canva AI offer automated layout options that enhance composition.
- o "Image Enhancement": AI-powered photo editing tools, such as Luminar Neo and Photoshop's Generative Fill, can enhance images by correcting colors, removing unwanted objects, and applying realistic effects, making the editing process faster and more intuitive.
- o "Brand Consistency": AI helps maintain brand identity by suggesting appropriate colors, fonts, and styles based on established guidelines, ensuring that all designs align with the brand's visual language.

"AI in Editing"

- o "Real-Time Feedback": AI tools can provide instant feedback on design elements, such as color balance and typography choices, helping editors refine their work quickly.
- o "Background Removal": AI can automate complex editing tasks like background removal, making it accessible for users of all skill levels. This feature is particularly useful for creating clean visuals for marketing materials.
- o "Image Upscaling": AI technologies like Topaz Gigapixel AI can upscale images without losing quality, making them suitable for high-resolution prints and digital displays.

"AI in Writing"

- o "Content Generation": AI writing assistants, such as ChatGPT, can help generate ideas, outlines, and even full drafts, streamlining the writing process for content creators.
- o "Grammar and Style Checking": Tools like Grammarly provide real-time feedback on grammar, punctuation, and style, helping writers improve their work before publication.
- o "Research Assistance": AI can assist in gathering relevant information and sources, making it easier for writers to support their arguments and enhance the quality of their content.

"Ease of Completing Work"

- o "Task Automation": AI can automate repetitive tasks across design, editing, and writing, allowing professionals to focus on more strategic and creative aspects of their work.
- o "User -Friendly Interfaces": Many AI tools offer intuitive interfaces that simplify the design and writing processes, making them accessible to users without extensive experience.
- o "Collaboration Features": AI-driven platforms facilitate collaboration among team members by organizing tasks, tracking progress, and providing a centralized space for feedback and revisions.
- o "Time Efficiency": By leveraging AI, professionals can complete projects faster, meet tight deadlines, and maintain high-quality standards without sacrificing creativity.

In summary, AI is revolutionizing graphic design, editing, and writing by enhancing creativity, automating tasks, and streamlining workflows. This allows professionals to focus on higher-level creative processes while improving efficiency and productivity across various projects.

- **Summary of Uses of AI**

Artificial Intelligence (AI) is transforming various industries by enhancing efficiency, improving decision-making, and automating tasks. Here's a summary of its key applications:

1. "Healthcare": AI aids in diagnostics through image analysis, predicts health outcomes with predictive analytics, and accelerates drug discovery by analyzing vast datasets.
2. "Finance": AI enhances fraud detection by analyzing transaction patterns, facilitates algorithmic trading for optimized investment strategies, and improves credit scoring through comprehensive data assessment.
3. "Retail": AI personalizes shopping experiences with tailored recommendations, optimizes inventory management by predicting demand, and provides 24/7 customer support through chatbots.
4. "Transportation": AI powers autonomous vehicles, optimizes traffic management to reduce congestion, and enhances route planning for logistics and delivery services.
5. "Manufacturing": AI enables predictive maintenance to prevent equipment failures, ensures quality control through computer vision, and optimizes supply chain operations.
6. "Education": AI personalizes learning experiences, provides intelligent tutoring systems for real-time feedback, and automates administrative tasks to allow educators to focus on teaching.
7. "Marketing": AI segments customers for targeted campaigns, generates marketing content, and conducts sentiment analysis to gauge public opinion on brands.
8. "Human Resources": AI streamlines recruitment by screening resumes, analyzes employee engagement data, and personalizes training programs for workforce development.
9. "Entertainment": AI recommends content on streaming platforms, enhances video game experiences with adaptive NPCs, and assists in scriptwriting for creative projects.
10. "Agriculture": AI supports precision farming by optimizing planting and harvesting, detects pests and diseases through image recognition, and monitors soil conditions for better crop management.

11. "Security": AI enhances surveillance with facial recognition, detects cybersecurity threats through network analysis, and prevents fraud in financial transactions.
12. "Smart Homes": AI automates home devices, powers voice assistants for hands-free control, and optimizes energy consumption for efficiency.

> Overall, AI is a versatile tool that is reshaping industries by improving processes, enhancing user experiences, and driving innovation across various sectors.

VI

How to Avoid Being Replaced by AI

As artificial intelligence (AI) continues to evolve and integrate into various sectors, many individuals express concerns about job displacement and the potential for AI to replace human roles. While it is true that AI can automate certain tasks, it is essential to recognize that AI is not poised to replace humans entirely. Instead, it is more likely to change the nature of work and the skills required to thrive in the workforce. This guide will explore strategies for staying relevant in the age of AI, focusing on developing irreplaceable skills, staying informed about AI advancements, and fostering a mindset of continuous learning.

Understanding the Impact of AI on Employment

1. The Nature of AI

AI is designed to perform specific tasks that involve data processing, pattern recognition, and automation. While AI excels in areas such as data analysis, repetitive tasks, and even some creative processes, it lacks the ability to replicate human qualities such as empathy, intuition, and complex problem-solving. Understanding the limitations of AI is crucial for recognizing the unique value that humans bring to the workplace.

> **Limitations of AI**

- "Lack of Emotional Intelligence": AI cannot understand or respond to human emotions in the way that people can. This limits its effectiveness in roles that require empathy, such as counseling, teaching, and customer service.
- "Contextual Understanding": AI systems often struggle with context. They can analyze data and recognize patterns but may misinterpret nuances in human communication or cultural references.
- "Creativity and Innovation": While AI can generate content and ideas based on existing data, it lacks the ability to think outside the box and create original concepts. Human creativity is driven by experiences, emotions, and intuition, which AI cannot replicate.

2. Job Transformation, Not Replacement

AI is more likely to transform jobs rather than eliminate them. Many roles will evolve to incorporate AI tools, requiring workers to adapt and learn how to work alongside these technologies. For example, data analysts may use AI to process large datasets more efficiently, allowing them to focus on interpreting results and making strategic decisions.

➤ **Examples of Job Transformation**
- "Healthcare": Radiologists may use AI to assist in diagnosing conditions from medical images, allowing them to focus on patient care and treatment planning rather than solely on image analysis.
- "Finance": Financial analysts can leverage AI tools to analyze market trends and generate reports, enabling them to provide more strategic insights to clients.
- "Marketing": Marketers can use AI to analyze consumer behavior and optimize campaigns, allowing them to focus on creative strategy and brand development.

3. The Importance of Human Skills

As AI takes over routine tasks, the demand for uniquely human skills will increase. Skills such as creativity, critical thinking, emotional intelligence, and interpersonal communication will become increasingly valuable in the workplace. These skills are difficult for AI to replicate and will be essential for collaboration, leadership, and innovation.

➤ **Key Human Skills to Develop**
- "Creativity": The ability to generate new ideas and solutions is invaluable in a world where innovation drives success. Engaging in creative activities, such as brainstorming sessions, artistic pursuits, or design thinking workshops, can enhance this skill.
- "Critical Thinking": The capacity to analyze information, evaluate evidence, and make informed decisions is crucial in navigating complex problems. Practicing logical reasoning, engaging in debates, and analyzing case studies can strengthen critical thinking abilities.
- "Emotional Intelligence (EQ)": Understanding and managing emotions, both in oneself and in others, is essential for effective communication and collaboration. Developing self-awareness, practicing empathy, and improving interpersonal skills can enhance EQ.
- "Adaptability": The ability to adjust to new situations and challenges is vital in a rapidly changing work environment. Embracing change, being open to new ideas, and cultivating a growth mindset can foster adaptability.

- **Strategies for Staying Relevant in the Age of AI**

1. Develop Skills That Are Difficult for AI to Replicate

> **Creativity**

Creativity is one of the most valuable skills in the age of AI. While AI can generate content and ideas, it lacks the ability to think outside the box and create original concepts. To enhance your creativity:

- "Engage in Creative Activities": Participate in activities that stimulate your imagination, such as writing, painting, or music composition. These activities can help you develop a unique perspective and innovative thinking.
- "Collaborate with Others": Work with diverse teams to gain new perspectives and ideas, fostering a creative environment. Brainstorming sessions and collaborative projects can lead to innovative solutions.
- "Embrace Failure": View failures as opportunities for growth and learning, which can lead to innovative solutions. Analyzing what went wrong and how to improve can enhance your creative problem-solving skills.

> **Critical Thinking**

Critical thinking involves analyzing information, evaluating evidence, and making informed decisions. To strengthen your critical thinking skills:

- "Question Assumptions": Challenge existing beliefs and consider alternative viewpoints to develop a well-rounded perspective. Engaging in discussions and debates can help refine your ability to think critically.
- "Analyze Case Studies": Study real-world examples to understand complex problems and the reasoning behind successful solutions. This practice can enhance your analytical skills and provide insights into effective decision-making.
- "Practice Problem-Solving": Engage in activities that require logical reasoning and problem-solving, such as puzzles or strategic games. These exercises can sharpen your ability to approach challenges methodically.

➢ **Emotional Intelligence**

Emotional intelligence (EQ) refers to the ability to understand and manage emotions, both in oneself and in others. To enhance your EQ:

- "Practice Self-Awareness": Reflect on your emotions and how they influence your behavior and decision-making. Keeping a journal can help you track your emotional responses and identify patterns.
- "Develop Empathy": Actively listen to others and try to understand their perspectives and feelings. Engaging in volunteer work or community service can provide opportunities to connect with diverse individuals and enhance your empathetic skills.
- "Improve Communication Skills": Work on expressing your thoughts and emotions clearly and constructively, fostering positive relationships. Participating in public speaking or communication workshops can help you become a more effective communicator.

2. Stay Up-to-Date on the Latest AI Developments

➢ **Follow Industry Trends**

Staying informed about AI advancements is crucial for understanding how they impact your field. To keep up with industry trends:

- "Subscribe to Newsletters": Follow reputable sources that cover AI developments, such as industry publications, blogs, and research organizations. This will help you stay informed about the latest innovations and applications of AI.
- "Attend Conferences and Webinars": Participate in events focused on AI and technology to learn from experts and network with peers. These gatherings can provide valuable insights into emerging trends and best practices.
- "Join Professional Associations": Engage with organizations related to your field that provide resources and insights on AI integration. Networking with professionals in your industry can help you stay connected and informed.

➤ Understand AI Applications in Your Industry

Different industries are adopting AI at varying rates and in different ways. To understand AI's impact on your field:

- "Research AI Use Cases": Investigate how AI is being utilized in your industry, including successful implementations and emerging trends. This knowledge can help you identify opportunities for leveraging AI in your work.
- "Network with AI Professionals": Connect with individuals working in AI-related roles to gain insights into their experiences and perspectives. Building relationships with AI experts can provide valuable guidance and mentorship.
- "Explore AI Tools": Familiarize yourself with AI tools and software relevant to your industry, and consider how they can enhance your work. Experimenting with these tools can help you become more proficient and adaptable.

2. Be Willing to Learn New Skills

➤ Embrace Lifelong Learning

The rapid pace of technological change necessitates a commitment to lifelong learning. To cultivate a growth mindset:

- "Set Learning Goals": Identify specific skills or knowledge areas you want to develop and create a plan to achieve them. Setting measurable goals can help you stay focused and motivated.
- "Take Online Courses": Utilize platforms like Coursera, Udemy, or LinkedIn Learning to access courses on AI, data analysis, and other relevant topics that can enhance your skill set. Online learning offers flexibility and a wide range of subjects.
- "Participate in Workshops": Attend hands-on workshops that provide practical experience with new technologies and methodologies. These experiences can deepen your understanding and application of new skills.

➤ Seek Feedback and Mentorship

Receiving feedback and guidance from others can accelerate your learning process. To benefit from mentorship:

- "Find a Mentor": Connect with someone experienced in your field or in AI who can provide insights and advice on navigating your career. A mentor can offer valuable perspectives and support your professional growth.
- "Request Constructive Feedback": Actively seek feedback on your work and skills from peers and supervisors to identify areas for improvement. Constructive criticism can help you refine your abilities and enhance your performance.

4. Cultivate Adaptability and Resilience

➤ Embrace Change

The ability to adapt to change is crucial in a rapidly evolving job market. To cultivate adaptability:

- "Stay Open-Minded": Be willing to explore new ideas, technologies, and ways of working. Embracing a mindset of curiosity can lead to new opportunities and insights.
- "Practice Flexibility": Develop a mindset that embraces change rather than resisting it, allowing you to pivot when necessary. Being flexible in your approach can help you navigate challenges more effectively.

➤ Build Resilience

Resilience is the capacity to recover from setbacks and maintain a positive outlook. To strengthen your resilience:

- "Develop Coping Strategies": Identify techniques that help you manage stress and maintain focus during challenging times. Mindfulness practices, such as meditation or yoga, can enhance your ability to cope with stress.
- "Foster a Support Network": Surround yourself with supportive colleagues, friends, and family who can provide encouragement and assistance. Building strong relationships can help you navigate difficult situations and maintain a positive mindset.

➢ Conclusion

In conclusion, while AI is set to transform the workforce, it is not an imminent threat to human employment. By focusing on developing irreplaceable skills, staying informed about AI advancements, and fostering a mindset of continuous learning, individuals can position themselves for success in the age of AI. Embracing creativity, critical thinking, emotional intelligence, and adaptability will not only enhance personal growth but also ensure relevance in an ever-changing job landscape. As we move forward, the collaboration between humans and AI will create new opportunities for innovation and progress, making it essential for individuals to prepare for this exciting future.

➢ Future Considerations

As we look ahead, it is important to consider the ethical implications of AI and its integration into society. Understanding the potential biases in AI algorithms, the importance of transparency, and the need for responsible AI development will be crucial for ensuring that technology serves humanity positively. Engaging in discussions about the ethical use of AI and advocating for policies that promote fairness and accountability will be essential for shaping a future where humans and AI coexist harmoniously.

➢ Final Thoughts

Ultimately, the key to thriving in the age of AI lies in recognizing the unique strengths that humans possess. By cultivating skills that complement AI technologies, remaining adaptable, and committing to lifelong learning, individuals can not only safeguard their careers but also contribute to a future where human creativity and innovation flourish alongside artificial intelligence. Embracing this journey with an open mind and a proactive approach will empower individuals to navigate the complexities of the modern workforce and seize the opportunities that lie ahead.

VII

The Benefits of
Using AI

Artificial Intelligence (AI) has emerged as a transformative force across various sectors, offering numerous benefits to individuals and businesses alike. As organizations increasingly adopt AI technologies, understanding the advantages they bring is crucial for leveraging their potential effectively. This comprehensive guide will explore the multifaceted benefits of using AI, focusing on increased efficiency, improved decision-making, enhanced creativity, cost reduction, enhanced customer experience, scalability, innovation, and competitive advantage, as well as addressing ethical considerations and challenges.

1. Increased Efficiency

1.1 Automation of Repetitive Tasks

One of the most significant benefits of AI is its ability to automate repetitive and time-consuming tasks. This automation allows employees to focus on more strategic and creative aspects of their work.

- "Examples of Automation":

  - "Data Entry": AI can automate data entry processes, reducing human error and freeing up time for employees to engage in more meaningful tasks. For instance, Optical Character Recognition (OCR) technology can convert scanned documents into editable text, streamlining data entry in various industries.

  - "Customer Support": AI-powered chatbots can handle routine customer inquiries, providing instant responses and allowing human agents to focus on complex issues. These chatbots can learn from interactions, improving their responses over time and enhancing customer satisfaction.

  - "Manufacturing": In manufacturing, AI-driven robots can perform repetitive tasks on assembly lines, increasing production speed and consistency. For example, automotive manufacturers use AI robots for tasks such as welding, painting, and assembly, resulting in higher efficiency and lower production costs.

1.2 Streamlined Workflows

AI can optimize workflows by analyzing processes and identifying bottlenecks. By streamlining operations, organizations can enhance productivity and reduce operational costs.

- "Process Optimization": AI tools can analyze workflow data to identify inefficiencies and suggest improvements. For example, AI can help logistics companies optimize delivery routes, reducing fuel consumption and delivery times. Companies like UPS use AI algorithms to analyze traffic patterns and weather conditions, allowing them to plan more efficient delivery routes.

- "Resource Allocation": AI can assist in resource management by predicting demand and allocating resources accordingly, ensuring that businesses operate at peak efficiency. For instance, AI can analyze historical sales data to forecast future demand, enabling retailers to optimize inventory levels and reduce stockouts.

1.3 Time Savings

By automating tasks and streamlining workflows, AI can significantly reduce the time required to complete projects. This time savings can lead to faster project delivery and increased overall productivity.

- "Project Management": AI-powered project management tools can automate scheduling, task assignments, and progress tracking, allowing teams to focus on execution rather than administrative tasks. Tools like Asana and Trello use AI to prioritize tasks based on deadlines and team member availability.

- "Data Analysis": AI can analyze large datasets in a fraction of the time it would take a human, providing insights that can inform decision-making and strategy development. For example, AI algorithms can process and analyze customer feedback from multiple sources, such as social media and surveys, to identify trends and areas for improvement.

2. Improved Decision-Making

2.1 Data-Driven Insights

AI excels at processing and analyzing vast amounts of data, enabling organizations to make informed decisions based on data-driven insights.

- "Predictive Analytics": AI can analyze historical data to identify trends and make predictions about future outcomes. For example, in finance, AI can predict stock market trends based on historical performance and market conditions. Companies like Bloomberg use AI to analyze financial data and provide investment recommendations to clients.

- "Real-Time Analysis": AI can provide real-time insights by continuously analyzing data streams. This capability is particularly valuable in industries such as healthcare, where timely information can impact patient outcomes. For instance, AI can monitor patient vital signs in real-time, alerting healthcare providers to any abnormalities that require immediate attention.

2.2 Enhanced Accuracy

AI algorithms can reduce human error in decision-making processes, leading to more accurate outcomes.

- "Risk Assessment": In finance and insurance, AI can assess risks more accurately by analyzing a broader range of factors than a human analyst might consider. This leads to better underwriting decisions and risk management strategies. For example, AI can analyze credit scores, transaction history, and social media activity to assess an individual's creditworthiness.

- "Quality Control": In manufacturing, AI can monitor production processes and identify defects in real-time, ensuring that products meet quality standards before reaching consumers. Companies like Siemens use AI-powered vision systems to inspect products on assembly lines, reducing defects and improving overall quality.

2.3 Scenario Analysis

AI can simulate various scenarios based on different variables, allowing organizations to evaluate potential outcomes and make informed decisions.

- "What-If Analysis": AI can conduct what-if analyses to assess the impact of different decisions on business outcomes. For example, a retailer can use AI to simulate the effects of changing pricing strategies on sales and profitability. This capability allows businesses to make data-driven decisions that align with their strategic goals.

- "Strategic Planning": AI can assist in strategic planning by analyzing market conditions, competitor behavior, and consumer preferences, helping organizations develop effective strategies for growth. For instance, AI can analyze social media trends and customer feedback to identify emerging market opportunities and inform product development.

3. Enhanced Creativity

3.1 Idea Generation

AI can serve as a valuable tool for idea generation, providing individuals and teams with new perspectives and inspiration.

- "Creative Collaboration": AI can analyze existing works in various fields, such as art, music, and writing, to generate new ideas and concepts. For example, AI algorithms can create music compositions based on different genres and styles, allowing musicians to explore new creative avenues.

- "Brainstorming Assistance": AI-powered tools can facilitate brainstorming sessions by suggesting ideas based on user inputs and preferences, helping teams overcome creative blocks. Tools like ChatGPT can generate prompts and suggestions that inspire creative thinking.

3.2 Design Assistance

In fields such as graphic design and architecture, AI can assist designers by generating design options and optimizing layouts.

- "Automated Design Tools": AI design tools can create multiple design variations based on user specifications, allowing designers to explore different aesthetics and functionalities quickly. For instance, platforms like Canva use AI to suggest design elements and layouts tailored to user preferences.

- "User Experience Optimization": AI can analyze user interactions with designs to provide insights on improving user experience, ensuring that designs are both visually appealing and functional. Companies like Adobe use AI to enhance their design software, enabling designers to create more intuitive and user-friendly interfaces.

3.3 Content Creation

AI can assist in content creation by generating written, visual, and multimedia content.

- "Writing Assistance": AI writing tools can help authors generate ideas, draft outlines, and even produce entire articles based on specified topics. These tools can analyze existing content to suggest improvements or alternative phrasing, enhancing the writing process. For example, tools like Grammarly and Jasper provide real-time feedback and suggestions to improve writing quality.

- "Visual Content Generation": AI can create images, videos, and graphics based on user inputs or existing styles. For instance, AI algorithms can generate artwork or design logos that align with brand identities, providing businesses with unique visual assets. Platforms like DALL-E allow users to create images from textual descriptions, expanding creative possibilities.

- "Personalized Content": AI can analyze user preferences and behaviors to create personalized content experiences. This capability is particularly valuable in marketing, where tailored content can significantly improve engagement and conversion rates. For example, streaming services like Netflix use AI to recommend shows and movies based on user viewing history.

4. Cost Reduction

4.1 Operational Cost Savings

By automating tasks and optimizing processes, AI can lead to significant cost savings for organizations.

- "Labor Cost Reduction": Automation of routine tasks can reduce the need for manual labor, allowing businesses to allocate resources more effectively. This can lead to lower operational costs and increased profitability. For instance, companies like Amazon use AI-driven robots in their warehouses to streamline order fulfillment, reducing labor costs and improving efficiency.

- "Error Reduction": AI's ability to minimize human error can lead to cost savings associated with rework, returns, and customer dissatisfaction. By ensuring higher accuracy in processes, organizations can avoid costly mistakes. For example, AI can help financial institutions reduce errors in transaction processing, leading to lower operational costs.

4.2 Resource Optimization

AI can help organizations optimize resource usage, leading to further cost savings.

- "Energy Efficiency": In industries such as manufacturing and logistics, AI can analyze energy consumption patterns and suggest optimizations to reduce energy costs. For example, AI can optimize machinery operation schedules to minimize energy use during peak hours, leading to significant cost savings.

- "Inventory Management": AI can predict demand and optimize inventory levels, reducing holding costs and minimizing waste. This is particularly important in retail, where overstocking can lead to markdowns and lost revenue. Companies like Walmart use AI to manage inventory levels, ensuring that products are available when customers need them while minimizing excess stock.

5.Enhanced Customer Experience

5.1 Personalized Interactions

AI can analyze customer data to provide personalized experiences, enhancing customer satisfaction and loyalty.

- "Tailored Recommendations": E-commerce platforms use AI algorithms to analyze customer behavior and preferences, offering personalized product recommendations that increase the likelihood of purchase. For example, Amazon's recommendation engine suggests products based on previous purchases and browsing history, driving sales and improving customer satisfaction.

- "Customized Marketing": AI can segment audiences based on behavior and preferences, allowing businesses to deliver targeted marketing campaigns that resonate with specific customer segments. This targeted approach can lead to higher engagement rates and improved conversion rates.

5.2 Improved Customer Support

AI-powered chatbots and virtual assistants can enhance customer support by providing instant responses and assistance.

- "24/7 Availability": AI chatbots can handle customer inquiries at any time , ensuring that customers receive support outside of regular business hours. This availability can improve customer satisfaction and reduce wait times. For instance, companies like Zendesk offer AI-driven customer support solutions that can handle a high volume of inquiries simultaneously.

- "Efficient Issue Resolution": AI can analyze customer queries and provide relevant solutions or escalate issues to human agents when necessary, ensuring that customers receive timely and effective support. This capability allows businesses to maintain high service levels while managing operational costs.

6. Scalability

6.1 Rapid Scaling of Operations

AI technologies can help businesses scale their operations quickly and efficiently.

- "Automated Processes": As businesses grow, AI can automate processes to handle increased workloads without the need for proportional increases in staff. This scalability allows organizations to expand without compromising quality or efficiency. For example, AI can manage customer interactions across multiple channels, ensuring consistent service as the customer base grows.

- "Data Handling": AI can manage and analyze large volumes of data, enabling organizations to scale their data-driven decision-making processes as they grow. This capability is essential for businesses that rely on data analytics to inform their strategies and operations.

6.2 Global Reach

AI can facilitate global operations by enabling businesses to operate in multiple markets simultaneously.

- "Language Translation": AI-powered translation tools can help businesses communicate with customers and partners in different languages, breaking down language barriers and expanding market reach. Companies like Google and Microsoft offer AI-driven translation services that enable real-time communication across languages.

- "Cultural Adaptation": AI can analyze cultural preferences and behaviors, allowing businesses to tailor their products and marketing strategies to resonate with diverse audiences. This adaptability is crucial for companies looking to enter new markets and connect with local consumers.

7. Innovation and Competitive Advantage

7.1 Driving Innovation

AI can drive innovation by enabling organizations to explore new ideas and solutions.

- "Research and Development": AI can analyze vast amounts of research data, identifying trends and gaps that can inform new product development. This capability accelerates the R&D process and fosters innovation. For instance, pharmaceutical companies use AI to analyze clinical trial data, speeding up drug discovery and development.

- "Collaboration with AI": By leveraging AI as a collaborative partner, organizations can explore creative solutions that may not have been possible through traditional methods. AI can assist in brainstorming sessions, providing insights and suggestions that enhance the creative process.

7.2 Gaining Competitive Advantage

Organizations that effectively integrate AI into their operations can gain a significant competitive edge.

- "Faster Time to Market": AI can streamline product development processes, allowing organizations to bring new products to market more quickly than competitors. For example, companies like Tesla use AI to optimize their manufacturing processes, enabling rapid production and delivery of electric vehicles.

- "Enhanced Customer Insights": By leveraging AI to analyze customer data, organizations can gain deeper insights into customer needs and preferences, enabling them to stay ahead of market trends. This understanding allows businesses to tailor their offerings and marketing strategies to meet evolving consumer demands.

8. Ethical Considerations and Challenges

8.1 Addressing Bias in AI

While AI offers numerous benefits, it is essential to address ethical considerations, particularly regarding bias in AI algorithms.

- "Bias Mitigation": Organizations must implement strategies to identify and mitigate bias in AI systems to ensure fair and equitable outcomes. This includes diversifying training data and regularly auditing AI algorithms for bias. For example, companies like IBM have developed frameworks to assess and reduce bias in AI models.

- "Transparency": Ensuring transparency in AI decision-making processes is crucial for building trust with customers and stakeholders. Organizations should communicate how AI is used and the rationale behind its decisions, fostering accountability and trust.

8.2 Data Privacy and Security

The use of AI often involves processing large amounts of personal data, raising concerns about privacy and security.

- "Data Protection": Organizations must prioritize data protection measures to safeguard customer information. Implementing robust cybersecurity protocols and adhering to data protection regulations, such as GDPR, is essential. Companies like Apple emphasize user privacy in their AI applications, ensuring that customer data is handled securely.

- "User Consent": Obtaining informed consent from users before collecting and processing their data is crucial for maintaining trust and compliance with legal standards. Organizations should clearly communicate their data collection practices and provide users with control over their information.

8.3 Job Displacement Concerns

While AI can enhance efficiency and productivity, it also raises concerns about job displacement.

- "Reskilling and Upskilling": Organizations should invest in reskilling and upskilling their workforce to prepare employees for new roles that emerge as AI technologies evolve. This proactive approach can help mitigate the impact of job displacement. Companies like Amazon have launched training programs to help employees transition to new roles in the AI-driven economy.

- "Creating New Opportunities": AI can also create new job opportunities in fields such as AI development, data analysis, and AI ethics, emphasizing the need for a balanced perspective on the future of work. As AI technologies advance, new roles will emerge that require human oversight, creativity, and emotional intelligence, which machines cannot replicate.

9. Conclusion

- ➤ The benefits of using AI are vast and varied, encompassing increased efficiency, improved decision-making, enhanced creativity, cost reduction, and a superior customer experience. As organizations continue to integrate AI technologies into their operations, understanding these advantages is crucial for maximizing their potential.
- ➤ However, it is equally important to address the ethical considerations and challenges associated with AI adoption. By prioritizing transparency, data privacy, and workforce development, organizations can harness the power of AI while ensuring a positive impact on society.
- ➤ In summary, AI is not just a tool for automation; it is a catalyst for innovation and growth. By embracing AI and its benefits, individuals and businesses can position themselves for success in an increasingly competitive landscape. As we move forward, the collaboration between humans and AI will shape the future of work, driving progress and creating new opportunities for all.

10. Final Thoughts

- ➤ The journey of AI is just beginning, and its potential to transform industries and improve lives is immense. As we embrace the benefits of AI, it is essential to remain vigilant about the ethical implications and challenges that accompany its adoption. By fostering a culture of innovation, collaboration, and responsibility, we can harness the power of AI to create a brighter future for all. The ongoing dialogue about AI's role in society will shape its trajectory, ensuring that it serves as a force for good in the world.

VIII

The Risks of Using AI

As artificial intelligence (AI) continues to permeate various aspects of our lives and industries, it brings with it a host of benefits, but also significant risks. Understanding these risks is crucial for individuals, organizations, and policymakers to navigate the complexities of AI deployment responsibly. This comprehensive guide will delve into the various risks associated with using AI, including job displacement, bias and discrimination, privacy concerns, security vulnerabilities, ethical dilemmas, and the potential for misuse.

1. Job Displacement

1.1 Overview of Job Displacement

Job displacement refers to the loss of jobs due to technological advancements, including automation and AI. As AI systems become more capable of performing tasks traditionally done by humans, there is a growing concern that many jobs may become obsolete.

> ➤ **Historical Context**

Historically, technological advancements have led to job displacement in various sectors. The Industrial Revolution, for example, saw many manual labor jobs replaced by machines. Similarly, the rise of computers and automation in the late 20th century led to significant changes in the workforce. AI represents the next wave of technological disruption, with the potential to impact a wide range of industries.

1.2 Sectors Most Affected

Certain sectors are more vulnerable to job displacement due to AI than others. These include:

- "Manufacturing": Automation and robotics have already transformed manufacturing processes, leading to the replacement of assembly line jobs. AI-driven robots can perform tasks such as welding, painting, and quality control with greater speed and precision than human workers.
- "Retail": AI technologies, such as self-checkout systems and automated inventory management, are reducing the need for cashiers and stock clerks. E-commerce platforms also leverage AI for personalized shopping experiences, impacting traditional retail jobs.
- "Transportation": The development of autonomous vehicles poses a significant threat to jobs in the transportation sector, including truck drivers, taxi drivers, and delivery personnel. Companies like Waymo and Tesla are actively working on self-driving technology that could disrupt the transportation industry.
- "Customer Service": AI-powered chatbots and virtual assistants are increasingly handling customer inquiries, reducing the need for human

customer service representatives. While these technologies can improve efficiency, they also raise concerns about job losses in the service sector.

1.3 The Nature of Job Displacement

Job displacement can occur in various forms, including:

- "Direct Displacement": This occurs when a job is entirely replaced by an AI system or automation. For example, a factory worker may lose their job to a robotic assembly line.
- "Indirect Displacement": This occurs when jobs are affected by changes in demand for certain skills or roles. For instance, as AI takes over routine tasks, the demand for low-skilled labor may decrease, leading to job losses in those areas.
- "Job Transformation": While some jobs may be displaced, others may evolve to incorporate AI technologies. Workers may need to adapt to new roles that require different skills, such as managing AI systems or interpreting data generated by AI.

1.4 Mitigating Job Displacement

To address the risks of job displacement, several strategies can be implemented:

- "Reskilling and Upskilling": Organizations should invest in training programs to help employees acquire new skills that are in demand in an AI-driven economy. This includes providing opportunities for workers to learn about AI technologies and how to work alongside them.
- "Lifelong Learning": Encouraging a culture of lifelong learning can help individuals stay relevant in the workforce. This involves promoting continuous education and professional development to adapt to changing job requirements.
- "Policy Interventions": Governments can play a role in mitigating job displacement by implementing policies that support workers affected by automation. This may include unemployment benefits, job placement services, and funding for retraining programs.

2. Bias and Discrimination

2.1 Overview of Bias in AI

Bias in AI refers to the presence of systematic and unfair discrimination in AI algorithms and systems. AI systems are trained on historical data, and if that data contains biases, the AI can perpetuate and even amplify those biases in its decision-making processes.

> ➤ Types of Bias
- "Data Bias": This occurs when the training data used to develop AI models is unrepresentative or skewed. For example, if an AI system is trained on data that predominantly features one demographic group, it may not perform well for individuals from other groups.
- "Algorithmic Bias": This occurs when the algorithms used in AI systems produce biased outcomes, even if the training data is unbiased. This can happen due to the design of the algorithm itself or the way it processes data.
- "Human Bias": Bias can also be introduced by the individuals who design and implement AI systems. If developers have unconscious biases, these can be reflected in the AI's behavior and decision-making.

2.2 Real-World Examples of Bias

Several high-profile cases have highlighted the risks of bias in AI systems:
- "Facial recognition technology": Studies have shown that facial recognition systems often have higher error rates for individuals with darker skin tones, leading to misidentification and wrongful accusations. For instance, a study by MIT Media Lab found that facial recognition algorithms misclassified the gender of darker-skinned women 34% of the time, compared to 1% for lighter-skinned men.
- "Hiring Algorithms": AI systems used in recruitment have been found to favor certain demographics over others. For example, an AI tool developed by Amazon was scrapped after it was discovered that it was biased against female candidates, as it was trained on resumes submitted over a ten-year period, which predominantly featured male applicants.

- "Predictive Policing": AI systems used in law enforcement to predict criminal activity have been criticized for perpetuating racial biases. These systems often rely on historical crime data, which can reflect systemic biases in policing practices, leading to over-policing in certain communities.

2.3 Addressing Bias in AI

To mitigate bias and discrimination in AI systems, several strategies can be employed:

- "Diverse Data Sets": Ensuring that training data is diverse and representative of the population can help reduce bias. This involves actively seeking out data from underrepresented groups and ensuring that AI systems are tested across various demographics.
- "Bias Audits": Regular audits of AI systems can help identify and address biases. Organizations can implement processes to evaluate the fairness of their AI algorithms and make necessary adjustments to improve outcomes.
- "Inclusive Development Teams": Building diverse teams of developers and data scientists can help bring different perspectives to the design and implementation of AI systems, reducing the likelihood of bias being introduced.

3. Privacy Concerns

3.1 Overview of Privacy Risks

AI systems often rely on vast amounts of data, including personal information, to function effectively. This raises significant privacy concerns, as individuals may not be aware of how their data is being collected, used, and shared.

> **Data Collection Practices**
- "Surveillance": AI technologies, such as facial recognition and tracking algorithms, can be used for surveillance purposes, leading to concerns about individual privacy and civil liberties. Governments and organizations may use these technologies to monitor citizens, raising ethical questions about consent and transparency.
- "Data Aggregation": AI systems can aggregate data from multiple sources, creating detailed profiles of individuals without their knowledge. This can lead to unauthorized use of personal information and potential breaches of privacy.

3.2 Regulatory Frameworks

The increasing use of AI has prompted calls for stronger regulatory frameworks to protect individuals' privacy. Key considerations include:

- "Data Protection Laws": Regulations such as the General Data Protection Regulation (GDPR) in the European Union aim to protect individuals' personal data and give them greater control over how their information is used. Similar laws are being considered in other regions to address privacy concerns related to AI.
- "Transparency Requirements": Organizations should be required to disclose how they collect, use, and share data, ensuring that individuals are informed about their data practices. This transparency can help build trust and accountability in AI systems.

3.3 Best Practices for Data Privacy

Organizations can adopt several best practices to enhance data privacy in AI systems:

- "Data Minimization": Collecting only the data necessary for a specific purpose can help reduce privacy risks. Organizations should evaluate their data collection practices and limit the information gathered to what is essential for their operations.

- "User Consent": Obtaining informed consent from individuals before collecting and processing their data is crucial. Organizations should clearly communicate their data practices and provide users with options to opt-out of data collection.
- "Robust Security Measures": Implementing strong cybersecurity measures can help protect personal data from unauthorized access and breaches. This includes encryption, access controls, and regular security audits.

4. Security Vulnerabilities

4.1 Overview of Security Risks

AI systems can be vulnerable to various security threats, including adversarial attacks, data breaches, and system failures. These vulnerabilities can have serious consequences for organizations and individuals.

> **Adversarial Attacks**
- "Manipulation of AI Models": Adversarial attacks involve manipulating input data to deceive AI systems. For example, slight alterations to images can cause a facial recognition system to misidentify individuals, leading to security breaches.
- "Data Poisoning": Attackers can introduce malicious data into the training set of an AI model, compromising its integrity and leading to biased or incorrect outcomes. This can undermine the reliability of AI systems in critical applications, such as healthcare and finance.

4.2 Data Breaches

The collection and storage of large amounts of personal data by AI systems increase the risk of data breaches. High-profile breaches can expose sensitive information, leading to identity theft and other security issues.

- "Impact of Data Breaches": Organizations that experience data breaches may face significant financial and reputational damage. The loss of customer trust can have long-term consequences for businesses, particularly in industries that rely on data privacy.

4 .3 Mitigating Security Risks

To address security vulnerabilities in AI systems, organizations can implement several strategies:

- "Robust Security Protocols": Establishing strong security measures, such as encryption, firewalls, and intrusion detection systems, can help protect AI systems from unauthorized access and attacks. Regular security assessments and updates are essential to maintain the integrity of these systems.
- "Adversarial Training": Incorporating adversarial training techniques can help AI models become more resilient to attacks. By exposing models to adversarial examples during training, organizations can improve their ability to withstand manipulation and enhance overall security.
- "Incident Response Plans": Developing comprehensive incident response plans can prepare organizations to respond effectively to security breaches. These plans should outline procedures for identifying, containing, and mitigating the impact of security incidents.

5. Ethical Dilemmas

• 5.1 Overview of Ethical Concerns

The deployment of AI raises numerous ethical dilemmas that organizations must navigate. These concerns often revolve around the implications of AI decision-making, accountability, and the potential for harm.

> **Accountability in AI Decision-Making**

- "Responsibility for Outcomes": When AI systems make decisions that lead to negative outcomes, questions arise about who is responsible. Is it the developers, the organizations using the AI, or the AI itself? Establishing clear accountability frameworks is essential to address these ethical dilemmas.
- "Transparency in Decision-Making": The 'black box' nature of many AI algorithms makes it challenging to understand how decisions are made. This lack of transparency can hinder accountability and trust, particularly in high-stakes applications such as healthcare and criminal justice.

5.2 Potential for Harm

AI systems can inadvertently cause harm, particularly when they are deployed without adequate oversight. Examples include:

- "Autonomous Weapons": The development of AI-powered weapons raises ethical concerns about the potential for misuse and the implications of delegating life-and-death decisions to machines. The lack of human oversight in such systems can lead to unintended consequences.
- "Misinformation and Manipulation": AI technologies, such as deepfakes and automated content generation, can be used to spread misinformation and manipulate public opinion. This poses significant risks to democratic processes and societal trust.

5.3 Addressing Ethical Dilemmas

To navigate ethical dilemmas associated with AI, organizations can adopt several approaches:

- "Ethical Guidelines": Developing and adhering to ethical guidelines for AI development and deployment can help organizations navigate complex ethical issues. These guidelines should prioritize fairness, accountability, and transparency.

- "Stakeholder Engagement": Involving diverse stakeholders, including ethicists, policymakers, and affected communities, in the development of AI systems can help ensure that ethical considerations are taken into account. This collaborative approach can lead to more responsible AI practices.

6. Potential for Misuse

6.1 Overview of Misuse Risks

The potential for misuse of AI technologies poses significant risks to individuals and society. Malicious actors can exploit AI for harmful purposes, leading to negative consequences.

- ➢ Cybersecurity Threats
- "Automated Cyber Attacks": AI can be used to automate and enhance cyber attacks, making them more sophisticated and difficult to detect. For example, AI algorithms can analyze vulnerabilities in systems and launch targeted attacks, increasing the risk of data breaches.
- "Phishing and Social Engineering": AI can be employed to create convincing phishing emails and social engineering tactics, making it easier for malicious actors to deceive individuals and gain unauthorized access to sensitive information.

6.2 Social Manipulation

AI technologies can be used to manipulate public opinion and behavior, raising ethical concerns about their impact on democracy and societal trust.

- "Targeted Misinformation Campaigns": AI can analyze social media data to identify and target specific demographics with tailored misinformation campaigns. This can influence public perception and behavior, undermining democratic processes.
- "Behavioral Manipulation": AI algorithms can be used to manipulate user behavior on platforms, such as social media and e-commerce sites, by exploiting psychological triggers. This raises ethical questions about consent and autonomy.

6.3 Mitigating Misuse Risks

To mitigate the risks of misuse, organizations and policymakers can implement several strategies:

- "Regulatory Frameworks": Establishing regulations that govern the use of AI technologies can help prevent misuse. This includes guidelines for responsible AI development and deployment, as well as penalties for malicious use.
- "Public Awareness Campaigns": Educating the public about the potential risks of AI misuse can empower individuals to recognize and respond to threats. Awareness campaigns can help build resilience against misinformation and manipulation.

7. The Risk of using Ai

The risks associated with using AI are multifaceted and complex, encompassing job displacement, bias and discrimination, privacy concerns, security vulnerabilities, ethical dilemmas, and the potential for misuse. As AI technologies continue to evolve, it is essential for individuals, organizations, and policymakers to address these risks proactively.

By implementing strategies to mitigate these risks, fostering transparency and accountability, and promoting ethical practices, we can harness the benefits of AI while minimizing its negative impacts. The future of AI will depend on our ability to navigate these challenges responsibly, ensuring that technology serves as a force for good in society.

8. Recommendations for Responsible AI Use

8.1 Establishing Ethical Frameworks

Organizations should develop and adopt ethical frameworks that guide the responsible use of AI. These frameworks should include principles such as fairness, accountability, transparency, and respect for user privacy. By adhering to these principles, organizations can foster trust and ensure that AI technologies are used in ways that benefit society.

8.2 Promoting Diversity and Inclusion

Diversity in AI development teams can help mitigate bias and discrimination in AI systems. Organizations should prioritize hiring practices that promote diversity and ensure that a wide range of perspectives is represented in the design and implementation of AI technologies. This can lead to more equitable outcomes and reduce the risk of bias in AI system.

8.3 Engaging Stakeholders

Engaging stakeholders, including affected communities, policymakers, and ethicists, in the development and deployment of AI technologies is crucial. This collaborative approach can help identify potential risks and ethical concerns early in the process, leading to more responsible AI practices.

8.4 Continuous Monitoring and Evaluation

Organizations should implement processes for continuous monitoring and evaluation of AI systems to identify and address biases, security vulnerabilities, and ethical concerns. Regular audits and assessments can help ensure that AI technologies are functioning as intended and that any issues are promptly addressed.

8.5 Fostering Public Awareness

Raising public awareness about the risks and benefits of AI is essential for promoting informed decision-making. Educational initiatives can help individuals understand how AI technologies work, the potential risks they pose, and how to protect their privacy and security in an increasingly AI-driven world.

9. The Role of Policymakers

9.1 Developing Regulatory Frameworks

Policymakers play a critical role in shaping the landscape of AI by developing regulatory frameworks that govern its use. These frameworks should address issues such as data privacy, accountability, and ethical considerations, ensuring that AI technologies are developed and deployed responsibly.

9.2 Supporting Research and Innovation

Governments should invest in research and innovation to advance the responsible development of AI technologies. This includes funding research on ethical AI, bias mitigation, and the societal impacts of AI, as well as supporting initiatives that promote collaboration between academia, industry, and government.

9.3 Encouraging International Cooperation

AI is a global phenomenon, and addressing its risks requires international cooperation. Policymakers should work together to establish global standards and best practices for AI development and deployment, ensuring that ethical considerations are prioritized across borders.

10. Conclusion

➤ As AI continues to evolve and integrate into various aspects of our lives, it is essential to recognize and address the associated risks. By fostering a culture of responsibility, transparency, and ethical considerations, we can harness the potential of AI while minimizing its negative impacts. The collaboration between individuals, organizations, and policymakers will be crucial in shaping a future where AI serves as a tool for positive change, driving innovation and improving the quality of life for all.

IX

How to Mitigate the

Risks of AI

As artificial intelligence (AI) continues to evolve and integrate into various aspects of society, it brings with it a range of risks, including job displacement, bias and discrimination, privacy concerns, security vulnerabilities, ethical dilemmas, and the potential for misuse. To harness the benefits of AI while minimizing its negative impacts, it is essential to implement strategies that mitigate these risks. This comprehensive guide will explore various approaches to mitigating the risks of AI, focusing on developing fair and unbiased AI systems, protecting individual privacy, creating jobs that are not easily automated, and fostering a culture of responsible AI use.

1. Developing Fair and Unbiased AI Systems

1.1 Understanding Bias in AI

Bias in AI refers to systematic and unfair discrimination in AI algorithms and systems. AI systems are trained on historical data, and if that data contains biases, the AI can perpetuate and even amplify those biases in its decision-making processes. Understanding the sources of bias is crucial for developing fair AI systems.

1.1.1 Types of Bias

- "Data Bias": This occurs when the training data used to develop AI models is unrepresentative or skewed. For example, if an AI system is trained on data that predominantly features one demographic group, it may not perform well for individuals from other groups. This can lead to significant disparities in outcomes, particularly in sensitive applications such as hiring, lending, and law enforcement.
- "Algorithmic Bias": This occurs when the algorithms used in AI systems produce biased outcomes, even if the training data is unbiased. This can happen due to the design of the algorithm itself or the way it processes data. For instance, if an algorithm is designed to prioritize certain features over others, it may inadvertently favor one group over another.
- "Human Bias": Bias can also be introduced by the individuals who design and implement AI systems. If developers have unconscious biases, these can be reflected in the AI's behavior and decision-making. This highlights the importance of diversity in AI development teams to mitigate the risk of human bias.

1.2 Strategies for Developing Fair AI Systems

To mitigate bias and discrimination in AI systems, several strategies can be employed:

1.2.1 Diverse Data Sets

Ensuring that training data is diverse and representative of the population can help reduce bias. This involves actively seeking out data from underrepresented groups and ensuring that AI systems are tested across various demographics.

- "Data Collection Practices": Organizations should implement data collection practices that prioritize diversity. This may involve collaborating with community organizations to gather data from underrepresented populations or using synthetic data to supplement existing datasets. For example, in facial recognition technology, ensuring that the training dataset includes a balanced representation of different ethnicities can help improve accuracy across diverse groups.
- "Data Audits": Regular audits of training data can help identify and address biases. Organizations should evaluate the composition of their datasets and make necessary adjustments to ensure that they reflect the diversity of the population. This can involve statistical analysis to assess representation and fairness in the data.

1.2.2 Bias Audits

Regular audits of AI systems can help identify and address biases. Organizations can implement processes to evaluate the fairness of their AI algorithms and make necessary adjustments to improve outcomes.

- "Algorithmic Audits": Conducting algorithmic audits involves testing AI systems for bias by analyzing their outputs across different demographic groups. This can help identify disparities in performance and inform necessary adjustments. For instance, an organization might analyze the outcomes of a hiring algorithm to ensure that it does not disproportionately favor one gender or ethnicity over another.
- "Third-Party Evaluations": Engaging third-party organizations to conduct independent evaluations of AI systems can provide an objective assessment of their fairness and effectiveness. This can enhance accountability and transparency in AI development. Third-party audits can also help build trust with stakeholders and the public.

1.2.3 Inclusive Development Teams

Building diverse teams of developers and data scientists can help bring different perspectives to the design and implementation of AI systems, reducing the likelihood of bias being introduced.

- "Diversity in Hiring": Organizations should prioritize diversity in their hiring practices, ensuring that teams reflect a wide range of backgrounds, experiences, and perspectives. This can lead to more equitable outcomes in AI development. For example, having team members from different cultural backgrounds can help identify potential biases in AI systems that may not be apparent to a homogenous team.
- "Training and Awareness": Providing training on bias and discrimination for AI developers can help raise awareness of potential biases and encourage more inclusive practices in AI design. This training can include workshops, seminars, and resources that educate developers about the importance of diversity and inclusion in AI.

1.3 Ethical Guidelines for AI Development

Establishing ethical guidelines for AI development can help organizations navigate complex ethical issues and promote fairness in AI systems.

1.3.1 Principles of Ethical AI

Organizations should adopt principles of ethical AI that prioritize fairness, accountability, transparency, and respect for user privacy. These principles can guide decision-making throughout the AI development process.

- "Fairness": AI systems should be designed to treat all individuals equitably, regardless of their demographic characteristics. This includes ensuring that AI algorithms do not discriminate against any group. Fairness can be operationalized through metrics that assess the performance of AI systems across different demographic groups.
- "Accountability": Organizations should establish clear lines of accountability for AI decision-making. This includes identifying who is responsible for the outcomes of AI systems and ensuring that there are mechanisms for addressing any negative impacts. Accountability frameworks can help organizations respond to issues that arise from AI use and provide recourse for affected individuals.

- "Transparency": AI systems should be transparent in their decision-making processes. Organizations should communicate how AI is used and the rationale behind its decisions, fostering trust and accountability. Transparency can be enhanced through explainable AI techniques that allow users to understand how decisions are made.

1.3.2 Stakeholder Engagement

Engaging diverse stakeholders in the development of AI systems can help ensure that ethical considerations are taken into account. This includes involving affected communities, policymakers, and ethicists in the design and implementation of AI technologies.

- "Community Involvement": Organizations should actively seek input from communities that may be affected by AI systems. This can help identify potential risks and ethical concerns early in the development process, leading to more responsible AI practices. Community engagement can take the form of focus groups, surveys, and public forums.
- "Public Consultations": Hosting public consultations and forums can provide a platform for stakeholders to voice their concerns and suggestions regarding AI technologies. This engagement can foster a sense of ownership and accountability among the community, ensuring that AI systems align with societal values.

2. Protecting the Privacy of Individuals

2.1 Understanding Privacy Risks

As AI systems often rely on vast amounts of personal data, privacy concerns are paramount. Individuals may not be aware of how their data is collected, used, and shared, leading to potential violations of privacy rights.

2.1.1 Data Collection Practices

- "Surveillance": AI technologies can be used for surveillance, raising ethical questions about consent and transparency. The use of facial recognition and tracking algorithms can infringe on individual privacy and civil liberties. Policymakers should consider regulations that limit the use of surveillance technologies in public spaces.
- "Data Aggregation": AI systems can aggregate data from multiple sources, creating detailed profiles of individuals without their knowledge. This can lead to unauthorized use of personal information and potential breaches of privacy. Organizations should be transparent about their data aggregation practices and provide individuals with options to control their data.

2.2 Strategies for Protecting Privacy

To mitigate privacy risks associated with AI, organizations can implement several strategies:

2.2.1 Data Minimization

Organizations should adopt data minimization practices, collecting only the data necessary for specific purposes. This reduces the risk of privacy violations and ensures that individuals' personal information is not unnecessarily exposed.

- "Purpose Limitation": Clearly defining the purpose for which data is collected can help organizations avoid collecting excessive information. This involves evaluating data needs regularly and adjusting practices accordingly. Organizations should communicate the purpose of data collection to individuals to enhance transparency.

- "Anonymization Techniques": Implementing anonymization techniques can help protect individual identities while still allowing organizations to analyze data. This includes removing personally identifiable information (PII) from datasets. However, organizations should be aware that anonymization is not foolproof and should implement additional safeguards.

2.2.2 User Consent

Obtaining informed consent from individuals before collecting and processing their data is crucial. Organizations should clearly communicate their data practices and provide users with options to opt-out of data collection.

- "Transparent Privacy Policies": Organizations should develop clear and accessible privacy policies that outline how data is collected, used, and shared. This transparency can help build trust with users. Privacy policies should be written in plain language and easily accessible.
- "Opt-In Mechanisms": Implementing opt-in mechanisms for data collection allows individuals to make informed choices about their privacy. This empowers users to control their data and enhances accountability. Organizations should provide users with clear options to manage their consent preferences.

2.2.3 Robust Security Measures

Implementing strong cybersecurity measures can help protect personal data from unauthorized access and breaches. This includes encryption, access controls, and regular security audits.

- "Data Encryption": Encrypting sensitive data can protect it from unauthorized access, ensuring that even if data is compromised, it remains unreadable without the appropriate decryption keys. Organizations should implement encryption protocols for data at rest and in transit.
- "Access Controls": Establishing strict access controls can limit who can access personal data within an organization. This reduces the risk of internal breaches and ensures that only authorized personnel can handle

sensitive information. Organizations should regularly review access permissions and implement role-based access controls.

3. Creating Jobs That Are Not Easily Automated

3.1 Understanding Job Automation

As AI technologies advance, there is a growing concern about job displacement due to automation. Certain jobs are more susceptible to being automated, particularly those that involve routine and repetitive tasks. Understanding which sectors are at risk and how to create resilient job opportunities is essential for mitigating the impact of automation.

3.1.1 Sectors at Risk

- "Manufacturing and Assembly": Jobs in manufacturing and assembly lines are highly susceptible to automation, as machines can perform these tasks more efficiently and accurately than human workers. The rise of robotics and AI in manufacturing has led to increased productivity but also significant job losses in traditional manufacturing roles.
- "Customer Service": AI-powered chatbots and virtual assistants are increasingly handling customer inquiries, reducing the need for human customer service representatives. While this can improve efficiency, it also raises concerns about job displacement for those in customer-facing roles.
- "Transportation and Delivery": The development of autonomous vehicles poses a significant threat to jobs in transportation and delivery services. Truck drivers, taxi drivers, and delivery personnel may face job losses as self-driving technology becomes more prevalent.

3.2 Strategies for Creating Resilient Jobs

To mitigate the risks of job displacement, it is essential to create jobs that are not easily automated. This involves focusing on roles that require human skills, creativity, and emotional intelligence.

3.2.1 Emphasizing Human-Centric Skills

Jobs that require human-centric skills, such as creativity, empathy, and critical thinking, are less likely to be automated. Organizations should prioritize the development of these skills in their workforce.

- "Training and Development": Providing training programs that focus on developing human-centric skills can help workers adapt to changing job requirements. This includes fostering creativity, problem-solving, and interpersonal skills. Organizations can partner with educational institutions to offer workshops and courses that enhance these skills.
- "Interdisciplinary Collaboration": Encouraging collaboration between different disciplines can lead to innovative solutions and job creation. For example, combining technology with the arts can result in new roles in creative industries, such as digital content creation and interactive design.

3.2.2 Promoting Lifelong Learning

Encouraging a culture of lifelong learning can help individuals stay relevant in the workforce. This involves promoting continuous education and professional development to adapt to changing job requirements.

- "Access to Education": Organizations should provide access to educational resources and training programs that enable employees to acquire new skills. This can include partnerships with educational institutions and online learning platforms that offer flexible learning options.
- "Career Pathways": Developing clear career pathways that outline opportunities for advancement can motivate individuals to pursue lifelong learning. This includes providing mentorship and support for skill development, helping employees navigate their career trajectories.

3.2.3 Supporting Entrepreneurship

Fostering entrepreneurship can create new job opportunities and drive economic growth. Encouraging individuals to start their own businesses can lead to the creation of jobs that are less susceptible to automation.

- "Access to Resources": Providing access to funding, mentorship, and resources for aspiring entrepreneurs can help them launch successful ventures. This includes offering grants, low-interest loans, and business development programs that support startups.
- "Innovation Hubs": Establishing innovation hubs and incubators can create environments where entrepreneurs can collaborate, share ideas, and develop new products and services. These spaces can foster creativity and drive job creation in emerging industries.

4. Fostering a Culture of Responsible AI Use

4.1 Understanding the Importance of Responsible AI

Fostering a culture of responsible AI use is essential for mitigating the risks associated with AI technologies. This involves promoting ethical practices, transparency, and accountability in AI development and deployment.

4.1.1 Ethical Considerations

- "Ethical AI Development": Organizations should prioritize ethical considerations in their AI development processes. This includes adhering to principles of fairness, accountability, and transparency, as well as engaging stakeholders in decision-making. Ethical AI development can help build public trust and ensure that AI technologies align with societal values.
- "Public Trust": Building public trust in AI technologies is crucial for their successful adoption. Organizations should communicate openly about their AI practices and demonstrate a commitment to ethical standards.

Transparency in AI development can help alleviate concerns about bias and discrimination.

4.2 Strategies for Promoting Responsible AI Use

To foster a culture of responsible AI use, organizations can implement several strategies:

4.2.1 Training and Awareness Programs

Providing training and awareness programs for employees can help them understand the ethical implications of AI and their role in promoting responsible practices.

- "Ethics Training": Organizations should offer training on ethical AI practices, including bias mitigation, data privacy, and accountability. This can help employees recognize potential risks and make informed decisions in their work. Training programs can include case studies, discussions, and interactive workshops.
- "Awareness Campaigns": Launching awareness campaigns that highlight the importance of responsible AI use can engage employees and encourage them to adopt ethical practices in their work. These campaigns can include informational materials, seminars, and discussions that emphasize the significance of ethical considerations in AI development.

4.2.2 Establishing Governance Frameworks

Implementing governance frameworks for AI development and deployment can help organizations ensure accountability and transparency in their practices.

- "AI Governance Committees": Establishing committees responsible for overseeing AI initiatives can help organizations maintain ethical standards and address potential risks. These committees should include diverse stakeholders to ensure a range of perspectives. Regular meetings can facilitate discussions on ethical dilemmas and decision-making processes.

- "Regular Reporting": Organizations should implement regular reporting mechanisms to track the performance and impact of AI systems. This can help identify potential issues and inform necessary adjustments. Reports should be made accessible to stakeholders to enhance transparency.

4.2.3 Engaging with External Stakeholders

Engaging with external stakeholders, including policymakers, ethicists, and community organizations, can help organizations navigate the complexities of AI deployment responsibly.

- "Collaborative Initiatives": Participating in collaborative initiatives with external stakeholders can foster knowledge sharing and promote best practices in AI development. This can lead to more responsible AI practices across industries. Joint projects can also help address common challenges and develop solutions.
- "Public Consultations": Hosting public consultations to gather input from affected communities can help organizations understand the potential impacts of their AI systems and address concerns proactively. This engagement can build trust and ensure that AI technologies align with community values.

5. Conclusion

> Mitigating the risks of AI is essential for harnessing its benefits while minimizing negative impacts on society. By developing fair and unbiased AI systems, protecting individual privacy, creating jobs that are not easily automated, and fostering a culture of responsible AI use, organizations can navigate the complexities of AI deployment effectively.

Implementing these strategies requires collaboration among individuals, organizations, and policymakers to ensure that AI technologies are developed and used responsibly. As AI continues to evolve, it is crucial to prioritize ethical considerations and promote practices that benefit society as a whole. The future of AI will depend on our ability to address these challenges proactively, ensuring that technology serves as a force for good in our lives.

6. The Role of Policymakers in Mitigating AI Risks

6.1 Developing Comprehensive Regulatory Frameworks

Policymakers play a critical role in shaping the landscape of AI by developing regulatory frameworks that govern its use. These frameworks should address issues such as data privacy, accountability, and ethical considerations, ensuring that AI technologies are developed and deployed responsibly.

6.1.1 Data Protection Regulations

Implementing robust data protection regulations is essential for safeguarding individual privacy in the age of AI. Policymakers should establish clear guidelines for data collection, storage, and usage, ensuring that individuals have control over their personal information.

- "General Data Protection Regulation (GDPR)": The GDPR serves as a model for data protection regulations worldwide. It emphasizes the importance of informed consent, data minimization, and individuals' rights to access and delete their data. Policymakers should consider adopting similar frameworks to enhance data protection.
- "Sector-Specific Regulations": Policymakers should consider developing sector-specific regulations that address the unique challenges posed by AI in different industries, such as healthcare, finance, and education. Tailored

regulations can help ensure that AI technologies are used responsibly in sensitive areas.

6.1.2 Accountability and Liability Frameworks

Establishing accountability and liability frameworks for AI systems is crucial for addressing ethical dilemmas and ensuring responsible AI use. Policymakers should clarify who is responsible for the outcomes of AI decision-making and establish mechanisms for addressing negative impacts.

- "Liability for AI Decisions": Policymakers should define liability for AI decisions, determining whether it rests with developers, organizations, or the AI systems themselves. This clarity can help ensure accountability and encourage responsible practices. Clear liability frameworks can also provide recourse for individuals affected by AI decisions.
- "Reporting Mechanisms": Implementing reporting mechanisms for AI-related incidents can help organizations identify and address issues promptly. This includes establishing channels for individuals to report concerns about AI systems, ensuring that organizations take accountability seriously.

6.2 Supporting Research and Innovation

Governments should invest in research and innovation to advance the responsible development of AI technologies. This includes funding research on ethical AI, bias mitigation, and the societal impacts of AI, as well as supporting initiatives that promote collaboration between academia, industry, and government.

6.2.1 Funding Ethical AI Research

Allocating funding for research on ethical AI practices can help organizations develop fair and unbiased systems. Policymakers should prioritize research initiatives that focus on bias mitigation, transparency, and accountability in AI technologies.

- "Grants for Ethical AI Projects": Providing grants for projects that explore ethical AI development can encourage innovation and promote responsible practices in the field. Funding can support interdisciplinary research that addresses the complexities of AI ethics.
- "Collaborative Research Initiatives": Supporting collaborative research initiatives between academia and industry can foster knowledge sharing and drive advancements in ethical AI practices. Partnerships can leverage diverse expertise and resources to tackle pressing challenges in AI development.

6.2.2 Promoting Public-Private Partnerships

Encouraging public-private partnerships can facilitate collaboration between government agencies and private organizations in the development of responsible AI technologies. These partnerships can leverage resources and expertise to address common challenges.

- "Joint Research Programs": Establishing joint research programs can enable organizations to work together on ethical AI initiatives, sharing best practices and resources to drive innovation. Collaborative projects can lead to the development of standards and guidelines that promote responsible AI use.
- "Innovation Hubs": Creating innovation hubs that bring together government, industry, and academia can foster collaboration and support the development of responsible AI technologies. These hubs can serve as incubators for new ideas and solutions, driving advancements in AI while ensuring ethical considerations are prioritized.

6.3 Encouraging International Cooperation

AI is a global phenomenon, and addressing its risks requires international cooperation. Policymakers should work together to establish global standards and best practices for AI development and deployment, ensuring that ethical considerations are prioritized across borders.

6.3.1 Global AI Governance Frameworks

Developing global AI governance frameworks can help establish common standards for ethical AI practices. Policymakers should collaborate with international organizations to create guidelines that promote responsible AI use worldwide.

- "International Agreements": Establishing international agreements on AI ethics and governance can facilitate cooperation among countries and promote the responsible development of AI technologies. These agreements can help align efforts to address shared challenges and risks associated with AI.
- "Cross-Border Data Regulations": Policymakers should work towards harmonizing data protection regulations across borders to ensure that individuals' privacy rights are upheld globally. This can enhance trust in AI technologies and facilitate international collaboration.

6.3.2 Sharing Best Practices

Encouraging the sharing of best practices among countries can help promote responsible AI development. Policymakers should facilitate platforms for knowledge exchange and collaboration on ethical AI initiatives.

- "Global Conferences and Workshops": Hosting global conferences and workshops on AI ethics can provide opportunities for stakeholders to share insights and experiences, fostering a collaborative approach to addressing AI risks. These events can bring together experts from various fields to discuss challenges and solutions.
- "Collaborative Research Networks": Establishing collaborative research networks can facilitate knowledge sharing and drive advancements in ethical AI practices across countries. These networks can support joint research initiatives and promote the dissemination of best practices.

7. Mitigating the risks of AI is essential for harnessing its benefits while minimizing negative impacts on society. By developing fair and unbiased AI systems, protecting individual privacy, creating jobs that are not easily automated, and fostering a culture of responsible AI use, organizations can navigate the complexities of AI deployment effectively.

> ➤ Policymakers play a crucial role in this process by establishing regulatory frameworks, supporting research and innovation, and encouraging international cooperation. The collaboration among individuals, organizations, and policymakers will be vital in shaping a future where AI serves as a tool for positive societal impact. As we move forward, it is imperative to prioritize ethical considerations and implement practices that ensure AI technologies contribute to the greater good, fostering a future where technology enhances human potential and well-being.

8. The Role of Education in AI Risk Mitigation

8.1 Integrating AI Ethics into Educational Curricula

Education plays a pivotal role in preparing future generations to navigate the complexities of AI technologies. Integrating AI ethics into educational curricula can equip students with the knowledge and skills necessary to develop and use AI responsibly.

8.1.1 Curriculum Development

- "Interdisciplinary Approach": Educational institutions should adopt an interdisciplinary approach to AI education, combining insights from computer science, ethics, sociology, and law. This can help students understand the multifaceted implications of AI technologies and the importance of ethical considerations in their development.

- "Case Studies and Real-World Applications": Incorporating case studies and real-world applications of AI can provide students with practical insights into the ethical dilemmas faced by organizations. Analyzing historical examples of AI failures can help students learn from past mistakes and develop critical thinking skills.

8.1.2 Training Educators

- "Professional Development": Providing professional development opportunities for educators can enhance their understanding of AI technologies and ethical considerations. Workshops, seminars, and online courses can help teachers stay informed about the latest developments in AI and its societal implications.
- "Resource Sharing": Creating platforms for educators to share resources, lesson plans, and best practices can foster collaboration and innovation in AI education. This can help ensure that students receive a comprehensive education that addresses the ethical dimensions of AI.

8.2 Promoting Digital Literacy

Digital literacy is essential for individuals to navigate the AI landscape effectively. Promoting digital literacy can empower individuals to understand AI technologies, their applications, and the associated risks.

8.2.1 Community Programs

- "Workshops and Training Sessions": Community organizations can offer workshops and training sessions focused on digital literacy and AI awareness. These programs can help individuals develop the skills needed to engage with AI technologies critically and responsibly.
- "Online Resources": Developing online resources, such as tutorials, articles, and videos, can provide accessible information about AI technologies and their implications. These resources can help individuals stay informed and make educated decisions regarding their interactions with AI.

8.2.2 Engaging Diverse Audiences

- "Targeting Underrepresented Groups": Efforts to promote digital literacy should prioritize underrepresented groups who may lack access to technology and education. Tailoring programs to meet the needs of diverse communities can help bridge the digital divide and ensure equitable access to AI knowledge.
- "Collaboration with Local Organizations": Partnering with local organizations, libraries, and community centers can enhance outreach efforts and provide individuals with opportunities to learn about AI technologies in supportive environments.

9. The Importance of Transparency in AI Development

9.1 Enhancing Transparency in AI Systems

Transparency is a critical component of responsible AI development. Enhancing transparency can help build trust among users and stakeholders, ensuring that AI technologies are developed and deployed ethically.

9.1.1 Explainable AI

- "Developing Explainable Models": Organizations should prioritize the development of explainable AI models that provide clear insights into how decisions are made. This can help users understand the rationale behind AI outputs and foster trust in the technology.
- "User -Friendly Interfaces": Creating user-friendly interfaces that present AI decision-making processes in an accessible manner can enhance transparency. Visualizations, summaries, and interactive tools can help users engage with AI systems more effectively.

9.1.2 Open Data Initiatives

- "Sharing Data and Algorithms": Organizations can promote transparency by sharing datasets and algorithms used in AI development. Open data initiatives can facilitate collaboration and allow researchers to validate and improve AI models.
- "Community Engagement": Engaging with the community to gather feedback on AI systems can enhance transparency and accountability. Organizations should actively seek input from users and stakeholders to ensure that AI technologies align with societal values.

9.2 Regulatory Transparency

- "Clear Guidelines and Standards": Policymakers should establish clear guidelines and standards for AI development that emphasize transparency. Regulations should require organizations to disclose information about their AI systems, including data sources, algorithms, and decision-making processes.
- "Public Reporting Requirements": Implementing public reporting requirements for AI systems can enhance accountability and transparency. Organizations should be required to disclose information about the performance and impact of their AI technologies, allowing stakeholders to assess their effectiveness.

10. Conclusion

- ➤ Mitigating the risks of AI is a multifaceted challenge that requires a comprehensive approach involving education, transparency, ethical guidelines, and collaboration among various stakeholders. By integrating AI ethics into educational curricula, promoting digital literacy, enhancing transparency in AI development, and fostering a culture of responsible AI use, we can navigate the complexities of AI technologies effectively.
- ➤ The collaboration among individuals, organizations, educators, and policymakers will be vital in shaping a future where AI serves as a tool for positive societal impact. As we move forward, it is imperative to prioritize ethical considerations and implement practices that ensure AI technologies contribute to the greater good, fostering a future where technology enhances human potential.

X

The Future of AI and Humans

The future of artificial intelligence (AI) is a topic of great interest and debate among technologists, ethicists, policymakers, and the general public. As AI continues to evolve and integrate into various aspects of our lives, it is essential to explore its potential impacts, the ethical considerations surrounding its use, and the collaborative relationship between humans and AI. This comprehensive guide will delve into the future of AI and humans, examining the opportunities and challenges that lie ahead, and proposing strategies for ensuring that AI is used responsibly and ethically for the benefit of humanity.

1. The Current State of AI

1.1 Overview of AI Technologies

AI encompasses a wide range of technologies, including machine learning, natural language processing, computer vision, and robotics. These technologies have made significant strides in recent years, leading to advancements in various fields such as healthcare, finance, transportation, and entertainment.

1.1.1 Machine Learning

Machine learning (ML) is a subset of AI that focuses on the development of algorithms that enable computers to learn from data and improve their performance over time. ML has been instrumental in driving advancements in AI, allowing systems to recognize patterns, make predictions, and automate tasks.

- "Supervised Learning": In supervised learning, algorithms are trained on labeled datasets, allowing them to make predictions based on input data. This approach is commonly used in applications such as image recognition and spam detection.
- "Unsupervised Learning": Unsupervised learning involves training algorithms on unlabeled data, enabling them to identify patterns and group similar data points. This approach is often used in clustering and anomaly detection.
- "Reinforcement Learning": Reinforcement learning involves training algorithms to make decisions based on feedback from their environment. This approach is commonly used in robotics and game-playing AI, where agents learn to optimize their actions to achieve specific goals.

1.1.2 Natural Language Processing

Natural language processing (NLP) is a branch of AI that focuses on the interaction between computers and human language. NLP enables machines to understand, interpret, and generate human language, facilitating communication between humans and AI systems.

- "Text Analysis": NLP techniques are used to analyze and extract insights from text data, enabling applications such as sentiment analysis, topic modeling, and information retrieval.
- "Conversational AI": NLP powers chatbots and virtual assistants, allowing them to engage in natural language conversations with users. This technology has transformed customer service and support, providing instant responses to inquiries.

1.1.3 Computer Vision

Computer vision is a field of AI that enables machines to interpret and understand visual information from the world. This technology has applications in various domains, including healthcare, security, and autonomous vehicles.

- "Image Recognition": Computer vision algorithms can identify and classify objects within images, enabling applications such as facial recognition and medical image analysis.
- "Object Detection": Object detection involves identifying and locating objects within images or video streams. This technology is used in surveillance systems, self-driving cars, and augmented reality applications.

1.1.4 Robotics

Robotics combines AI with physical machines to create autonomous systems capable of performing tasks in the real world. AI-powered robots are increasingly being used in manufacturing, healthcare, logistics, and other industries.

- "Industrial Automation": AI-driven robots are used in manufacturing to automate repetitive tasks, improving efficiency and reducing labor costs. These robots can work alongside human workers, enhancing productivity.
- "Service Robots": Service robots, such as delivery drones and robotic assistants, are being deployed in various sectors to perform tasks that require mobility and interaction with the environment.

1.2 Current Applications of AI

AI technologies are already being applied across various sectors, transforming industries and improving efficiency. Some notable applications include:

- "Healthcare": AI is used for diagnostics, predictive analytics, and personalized medicine. For example, AI algorithms can analyze medical images to detect diseases, while predictive models can forecast patient outcomes based on historical data.
- "Finance": AI is employed in fraud detection, algorithmic trading, and risk assessment. Financial institutions use AI to analyze transaction patterns and identify anomalies, helping to prevent fraud.
- "Transportation": AI powers autonomous vehicles, optimizing navigation and decision-making. Ride-sharing platforms use AI algorithms to match drivers with passengers and optimize routes.
- "Retail": AI enhances customer experiences through personalized recommendations, inventory management, and demand forecasting. E-commerce platforms leverage AI to analyze customer behavior and tailor marketing strategies.
- "Entertainment": AI is used in content recommendation systems, video game development, and content creation. Streaming services like Netflix use AI algorithms to suggest shows and movies based on user preferences.

2. The Potential of AI in the Future

2.1 Transformative Opportunities

The future of AI holds transformative opportunities that can significantly impact various aspects of society. These opportunities include:

2.1.1 Enhanced Productivity

AI has the potential to enhance productivity across industries by automating routine tasks and enabling workers to focus on higher-value activities. By streamlining processes and improving efficiency, AI can lead to increased output and innovation.

- "Automation of Repetitive Tasks": AI can take over mundane and repetitive tasks, allowing employees to dedicate their time to more complex and creative endeavors. For instance, in manufacturing, AI-driven robots can handle assembly line work, freeing human workers to engage in quality control and process improvement.
- "Augmented Decision-Making": AI can assist in decision-making by providing data-driven insights and predictive analytics. This can empower organizations to make informed choices, optimize operations, and respond swiftly to market changes.

2.1.2 Improved Quality of Life

AI has the potential to improve the quality of life for individuals by enhancing healthcare, education, and accessibility.

- "Personalized Healthcare": AI can analyze vast amounts of medical data to provide personalized treatment plans and early diagnosis of diseases. This can lead to better health outcomes and more efficient use of healthcare resources.
- "Accessible Education": AI-powered educational tools can provide personalized learning experiences, adapting to the needs and learning styles of individual students. This can help bridge educational gaps and improve learning outcomes.
- "Smart Assistive Technologies": AI can enhance accessibility for individuals with disabilities through smart assistive technologies, such as voice recognition software and smart home devices that respond to user commands.

2.1.3 Environmental Sustainability

AI can play a crucial role in addressing environmental challenges by optimizing resource use and promoting sustainable practices.

- "Energy Management": AI can optimize energy consumption in buildings and industries, reducing waste and lowering carbon footprints. Smart grids powered by AI can manage energy distribution more efficiently, integrating renewable energy sources.
- "Climate Modeling": AI can enhance climate modeling and prediction, helping scientists understand climate change impacts and develop strategies for mitigation and adaptation.
- "Sustainable Agriculture": AI technologies can improve agricultural practices through precision farming, optimizing water usage, and reducing pesticide application, leading to more sustainable food production.

2.2 Challenges and Risks

While the future of AI presents numerous opportunities, it also poses significant challenges and risks that must be addressed.

2.2.1 Ethical Concerns

The ethical implications of AI technologies are a major concern, particularly regarding bias, discrimination, and accountability.

- "Bias in AI Systems": AI algorithms can perpetuate existing biases present in training data, leading to unfair outcomes in areas such as hiring, lending, and law enforcement. Addressing bias in AI systems is essential to ensure fairness and equity.
- "Accountability for AI Decisions": As AI systems become more autonomous, determining accountability for their decisions becomes complex. Establishing clear frameworks for accountability is crucial to address potential harms caused by AI.

2.2.2 Job Displacement

The automation of tasks through AI may lead to job displacement in certain sectors, raising concerns about unemployment and economic inequality.

- "Reskilling and Upskilling": To mitigate the impact of job displacement, it is essential to invest in reskilling and upskilling programs that prepare workers for new roles in an AI-driven economy. This includes providing access to training and education in emerging fields.
- "Creating New Job Opportunities": While AI may displace certain jobs, it can also create new opportunities in areas such as AI development, data analysis, and ethical oversight. Fostering innovation and entrepreneurship can help generate new employment avenues.

2.2.3 Privacy and Security

The use of AI often involves the collection and analysis of vast amounts of personal data, raising concerns about privacy and security.

- "Data Protection Regulations": Implementing robust data protection regulations is essential to safeguard individuals' privacy rights. Organizations must prioritize transparency in data collection and usage practices.
- "Cybersecurity Risks": AI systems can be vulnerable to cyberattacks, which can compromise sensitive data and disrupt operations. Strengthening cybersecurity measures is crucial to protect AI systems from malicious threats.

3. The Collaborative Future of Humans and AI

3.1 Human-AI Collaboration

The future of AI will likely involve a collaborative relationship between humans and AI systems, where both can complement each other's strengths.

3.1.1 Augmented Intelligence

Rather than replacing humans, AI can augment human intelligence by providing tools and insights that enhance decision-making and creativity.

- "Human-Centric AI Design": Designing AI systems with a focus on human needs and capabilities can lead to more effective collaboration. This includes creating user-friendly interfaces and ensuring that AI systems are interpretable and explainable.
- "Empowering Workers": AI can empower workers by providing them with data-driven insights and automating routine tasks, allowing them to focus on strategic and creative aspects of their work.

3.1.2 Ethical AI Development

Ensuring that AI technologies are developed ethically is essential for fostering trust and collaboration between humans and AI.

- "Inclusive Development Teams": Building diverse teams of developers and stakeholders can help identify and address potential biases in AI systems. - "Stakeholder Engagement": Engaging with various stakeholders, including affected communities and ethicists, can provide valuable insights into the ethical implications of AI technologies. This collaborative approach can help ensure that AI systems align with societal values and priorities.

3.2 Education and Training for the Future

Preparing the workforce for a future where AI plays a significant role requires a focus on education and training.

3.2.1 Curriculum Innovation

Educational institutions should adapt their curricula to include AI literacy, ethics, and interdisciplinary studies that combine technology with social sciences.

- "AI Literacy Programs": Introducing AI literacy programs at all educational levels can help individuals understand AI technologies, their applications, and their implications. This knowledge will empower future generations to engage critically with AI.
- "Interdisciplinary Learning": Encouraging interdisciplinary learning can foster a holistic understanding of AI's impact on society. Students should be exposed to the ethical, social, and economic dimensions of AI alongside technical skills.

3.2.2 Lifelong Learning Initiatives

As the job market evolves, promoting a culture of lifelong learning will be essential for individuals to adapt to changing demands.

- "Access to Continuous Education": Organizations and governments should provide access to continuous education and training programs that enable workers to acquire new skills and stay relevant in an AI-driven economy.
- "Mentorship and Support": Establishing mentorship programs can help individuals navigate their career paths and develop the skills needed to thrive in a rapidly changing job landscape.

4. Policy and Governance for AI

4.1 Regulatory Frameworks

Developing comprehensive regulatory frameworks for AI is crucial to ensure its responsible use and mitigate potential risks.

4.1.1 Ethical Guidelines

Policymakers should establish ethical guidelines for AI development and deployment that prioritize fairness, accountability, and transparency.

- "AI Ethics Boards": Creating independent AI ethics boards can provide oversight and guidance on ethical considerations in AI development. These boards should include diverse stakeholders to ensure a range of perspectives.
- "Public Accountability": Implementing mechanisms for public accountability can help ensure that organizations are held responsible for the ethical implications of their AI systems. This includes requiring organizations to report on their AI practices and outcomes.

4.1.2 International Cooperation

Given the global nature of AI, international cooperation is essential for establishing common standards and best practices.

- "Global AI Governance": Collaborating with international organizations to develop global AI governance frameworks can help promote responsible AI practices across borders. This includes harmonizing regulations and sharing best practices.
- "Cross-Border Data Regulations": Policymakers should work towards establishing cross-border data regulations that protect individuals' privacy rights while facilitating the responsible use of AI technologies.

5. The future of AI and humans

The future of AI and humans is filled with both opportunities and challenges. By embracing a collaborative approach that prioritizes ethical considerations, education, and responsible governance, we can harness the transformative potential of AI for the benefit of humanity. As we navigate this evolving landscape, it is essential to foster a culture of innovation, inclusivity, and accountability, ensuring that AI technologies contribute positively to society and enhance the human experience. The journey ahead will require collective efforts from individuals, organizations, and policymakers to shape a future where AI serves as a powerful ally in addressing the complex challenges of our time.

6. The Role of AI in Addressing Global Challenges

6.1 Tackling Climate Change

AI has the potential to play a significant role in combating climate change by optimizing resource use, enhancing energy efficiency, and supporting sustainable practices.

6.1.1 Climate Modeling and Prediction

AI can improve climate modeling and prediction by analyzing vast datasets to identify patterns and trends. This can help scientists understand the impacts of climate change and develop effective mitigation strategies.

- "Data-Driven Insights": Machine learning algorithms can analyze historical climate data to predict future climate scenarios, enabling policymakers to make informed decisions regarding climate action.

- "Real-Time Monitoring": AI-powered sensors and satellite imagery can provide real-time monitoring of environmental changes, such as deforestation and pollution levels, allowing for timely interventions.

6.1.2 Energy Efficiency

AI can optimize energy consumption in various sectors, reducing waste and promoting sustainability.

- "Smart Grids": AI can enhance the efficiency of smart grids by predicting energy demand and optimizing energy distribution. This can facilitate the integration of renewable energy sources and reduce reliance on fossil fuels.
- "Building Management Systems": AI-driven building management systems can optimize heating, cooling, and lighting based on occupancy patterns, leading to significant energy savings.

6.2 Enhancing Healthcare Delivery

AI has the potential to revolutionize healthcare delivery by improving diagnostics, treatment, and patient care.

6.2.1 Precision Medicine

AI can analyze genetic, environmental, and lifestyle data to provide personalized treatment plans tailored to individual patients.

- "Genomic Analysis": AI algorithms can process genomic data to identify genetic markers associated with diseases, enabling targeted therapies and improved patient outcomes.
- "Predictive Analytics": AI can predict patient outcomes based on historical data, allowing healthcare providers to intervene early and improve care.

6.2.2 Telemedicine and Remote Monitoring

AI can enhance telemedicine and remote monitoring, making healthcare more accessible and efficient.

- "Virtual Health Assistants": AI-powered virtual health assistants can provide patients with personalized health information and support, improving engagement and adherence to treatment plans.
- "Remote Patient Monitoring": AI can analyze data from wearable devices to monitor patients' health in real-time, enabling timely interventions and reducing hospital readmissions.

6.3 Improving Education and Learning

AI can transform education by providing personalized learning experiences and enhancing access to educational resources.

6.3.1 Adaptive Learning Technologies

AI can create adaptive learning platforms that tailor educational content to individual students' needs and learning styles.

- "Personalized Learning Paths": AI algorithms can analyze students' performance and preferences to create customized learning paths, ensuring that each student receives the support they need to succeed.
- "Intelligent Tutoring Systems": AI-powered tutoring systems can provide real-time feedback and guidance, helping students master complex concepts and improve their skills.

6.3.2 Expanding Access to Education

AI can help bridge educational gaps by providing access to quality learning resources for underserved communities.

- "Online Learning Platforms": AI can enhance online learning platforms by recommending relevant courses and resources based on students' interests and goals, making education more accessible.

- "Language Translation": AI-driven language translation tools can facilitate communication and learning for non-native speakers, breaking down language barriers in education.

7. The Ethical Implications of AI

7.1 Addressing Bias and Discrimination

As AI systems become more prevalent, addressing bias and discrimination in AI algorithms is crucial to ensure fairness and equity.

7.1.1 Identifying Sources of Bias

Understanding the sources of bias in AI systems is essential for developing fair algorithms.

- "Data Bias": AI systems trained on biased datasets can perpetuate existing inequalities. Organizations must ensure that training data is diverse and representative of the population.
- "Algorithmic Bias": Bias can also arise from the design of algorithms themselves. Developers should prioritize fairness in algorithm design and regularly audit AI systems for biased outcomes.

7.1.2 Implementing Fairness Metrics

Establishing fairness metrics can help organizations assess the performance of AI systems across different demographic groups.

- "Equity Metrics": Organizations should develop equity metrics that evaluate the impact of AI systems on various demographic groups, ensuring that no group is disproportionately affected by negative outcomes.
- "Regular Audits": Conducting regular audits of AI systems can help identify and address biases, promoting accountability and transparency in AI development.

7.2 Ensuring Accountability and Transparency

Establishing accountability and transparency in AI systems is essential for building trust and ensuring responsible use.

7.2.1 Clear Accountability Frameworks

Organizations should establish clear accountability frameworks for AI decision-making.

- "Defining Responsibility": Policymakers should clarify who is responsible for the outcomes of AI systems, whether it be developers, organizations, or the AI systems themselves.
- "Reporting Mechanisms": Implementing reporting mechanisms for AI-related incidents can help organizations identify and address issues promptly . This includes establishing channels for individuals to report concerns about AI systems, ensuring that organizations take accountability seriously.

7.2.2 Promoting Transparency in AI Development

Transparency is crucial for fostering trust in AI technologies. Organizations should prioritize transparency in their AI development processes.

- "Open Communication": Organizations should communicate openly about their AI practices, including data sources, algorithms, and decision-making processes. This transparency can help alleviate concerns about bias and discrimination.

- "Explainable AI": Developing explainable AI models that provide clear insights into how decisions are made can enhance transparency. Users should be able to understand the rationale behind AI outputs, fostering trust in the technology.

8. The Future of Work in an AI-Driven World

8.1 Evolving Job Roles

As AI technologies continue to advance, the nature of work will evolve, leading to the emergence of new job roles and the transformation of existing ones.

8.1.1 New Job Opportunities

AI is expected to create new job opportunities in various fields, particularly in technology, data analysis, and AI ethics.

- "AI Development and Maintenance": As organizations adopt AI technologies, there will be a growing demand for professionals skilled in AI development, data science, and machine learning.
- "Ethical Oversight": The need for ethical oversight in AI development will create roles focused on ensuring that AI systems are developed and used responsibly.

8.1.2 Transformation of Existing Roles

Many existing job roles will be transformed as AI automates routine tasks and enhances decision-making.

- "Augmented Roles": Workers in various industries will find their roles augmented by AI, allowing them to focus on higher-value tasks that require creativity, critical thinking, and emotional intelligence.
- "Collaboration with AI": Employees will increasingly collaborate with AI systems, leveraging their capabilities to improve productivity and efficiency.

8.2 Reskilling and Upskilling

To prepare for the future of work, organizations and individuals must prioritize reskilling and upskilling initiatives.

8.2.1 Lifelong Learning Culture

Fostering a culture of lifelong learning is essential for individuals to adapt to changing job requirements.

- "Access to Training Programs": Organizations should provide access to training programs that enable employees to acquire new skills and stay relevant in an AI-driven economy.
- "Mentorship Opportunities": Establishing mentorship programs can help individuals navigate their career paths and develop the skills needed to thrive in a rapidly changing job landscape.

8.2.2 Collaboration with Educational Institutions

Partnerships between organizations and educational institutions can enhance training initiatives and ensure that curricula align with industry needs.

- "Curriculum Development": Collaborating with educational institutions to develop curricula that address the skills needed in an AI-driven workforce can help bridge the skills gap.

- "Internship and Apprenticeship Programs": Offering internship and apprenticeship programs can provide individuals with hands-on experience in AI technologies and prepare them for future job opportunities.

9. The Role of Government in AI Governance

9.1 Establishing Regulatory Frameworks

Governments play a crucial role in establishing regulatory frameworks that govern the use of AI technologies.

9.1.1 Comprehensive AI Policies

Developing comprehensive AI policies that address ethical considerations, data protection, and accountability is essential for responsible AI use.

- "Ethical Guidelines": Policymakers should establish ethical guidelines for AI development and deployment that prioritize fairness, accountability, and transparency.
- "Data Protection Regulations": Implementing robust data protection regulations is essential to safeguard individuals' privacy rights in the age of AI.

9.1.2 International Cooperation

Given the global nature of AI, international cooperation is essential for establishing common standards and best practices.

- "Global AI Governance": Collaborating with international organizations to develop global AI governance frameworks can help promote responsible AI practices across borders.

- "Cross-Border Data Regulations": Policymakers should work towards establishing cross-border data regulations that protect individuals' privacy rights while facilitating the responsible use of AI technologies.

10. Conclusion

The future of AI and humans is filled with both opportunities and challenges. By embracing a collaborative approach that prioritizes ethical considerations, education, and responsible governance, we can harness the transformative potential of AI for the benefit of humanity. As we navigate this evolving landscape, it is essential to foster a culture of innovation, inclusivity, and accountability, ensuring that AI technologies contribute positively to society and enhance the human experience. The journey ahead will require collective efforts from individuals, organizations, and policymakers to shape a future where AI serves as a powerful ally in addressing the complex challenges of our time.

- **Conclusion: The Dual Nature of AI and Its Impact on Humanity**

> ➢ Artificial Intelligence (AI) stands as one of the most transformative technologies of our time, with the potential to reshape industries, enhance human capabilities, and address some of the world's most pressing challenges. However, like any powerful tool, AI carries with it the dual potential for both positive and negative outcomes. As we navigate the complexities of AI's integration into society, it is crucial to recognize the importance of responsible and ethical use to ensure that AI serves the greater good.

1. The Power of AI

1.1 Transformative Potential

AI has the capacity to revolutionize various sectors, including healthcare, education, finance, transportation, and more. Its ability to analyze vast amounts of data, recognize patterns, and make predictions can lead to significant advancements in efficiency, productivity, and innovation.

- "Healthcare": AI can enhance diagnostics, personalize treatment plans, and improve patient outcomes. For instance, AI algorithms can analyze medical images to detect diseases at earlier stages, leading to timely interventions and better health management.
- "Education": AI can provide personalized learning experiences, adapting to individual students' needs and learning styles. This can help bridge educational gaps and improve learning outcomes for diverse populations.
- "Finance": AI can optimize trading strategies, detect fraudulent activities, and enhance risk assessment. Financial institutions can leverage AI to analyze market trends and make data-driven investment decisions.

1.2 Addressing Global Challenges

AI also holds promise in addressing global challenges such as climate change, poverty, and public health crises. By harnessing AI's capabilities, we can develop innovative solutions to complex problems.

- "Climate Change": AI can optimize energy consumption, enhance climate modeling, and support sustainable practices in agriculture and resource management. For example, AI can analyze weather patterns to improve crop yields and reduce waste.
- "Disaster Response": AI can assist in disaster response efforts by analyzing data from various sources to predict natural disasters and coordinate relief efforts. This can save lives and minimize the impact of catastrophic events.

2. The Risks of AI

2.1 Job Displacement

One of the most significant concerns surrounding AI is the potential for job displacement. As AI systems become capable of performing tasks traditionally done by humans, there is a risk that many jobs may become obsolete.

- "Automation of Routine Tasks": AI can automate repetitive and mundane tasks, leading to job losses in sectors such as manufacturing, retail, and customer service. While automation can improve efficiency, it also raises concerns about unemployment and economic inequality.
- "Need for Reskilling": To mitigate the impact of job displacement, it is essential to invest in reskilling and upskilling initiatives that prepare workers for new roles in an AI-driven economy. This includes providing access to training programs that focus on developing human-centric skills.

2.2 Bias and Discrimination

AI systems can perpetuate existing biases present in training data, leading to unfair and discriminatory outcomes. This is particularly concerning in sensitive applications such as hiring, lending, and law enforcement.

- "Data Bias": If AI systems are trained on biased datasets, they may produce biased results. For example, facial recognition technology has been shown to have higher error rates for individuals with darker skin tones, leading to misidentification and wrongful accusations.
- "Algorithmic Bias": Bias can also arise from the design of algorithms themselves. Developers must prioritize fairness in algorithm design and regularly audit AI systems for biased outcomes to ensure equitable treatment.

2.3 Privacy Concerns

The use of AI often involves the collection and analysis of vast amounts of personal data, raising significant privacy concerns.

- "Data Collection Practices": AI systems can aggregate data from multiple sources, creating detailed profiles of individuals without their knowledge. This can lead to unauthorized use of personal information and potential breaches of privacy.
- "Surveillance": AI technologies can be used for surveillance, raising ethical questions about consent and transparency. The use of facial recognition and tracking algorithms can infringe on individual privacy and civil liberties.

3. The Importance of Responsible and Ethical AI Use

3.1 Ethical Guidelines

To harness the benefits of AI while mitigating its risks, it is essential to establish ethical guidelines for AI development and deployment. These guidelines should prioritize fairness, accountability, transparency, and respect for user privacy.

- "Fairness": AI systems should be designed to treat all individuals equitably, regardless of their demographic characteristics. This includes ensuring that AI algorithms do not discriminate against any group.
- "Accountability": Organizations should establish clear lines of accountability for AI decision-making. This includes identifying who is responsible for the outcomes of AI systems and ensuring that there are mechanisms for addressing any negative impacts.
- "Transparency": AI systems should be transparent in their decision-making processes. Organizations should communicate how AI is used and the rationale behind its decisions, fostering trust and accountability.

3.2 Stakeholder Engagement

Engaging diverse stakeholders in the development of AI systems can help ensure that ethical considerations are taken into account. This includes involving affected communities, policymakers, and ethicists in the design and implementation of AI technologies.

- "Community Involvement": Organizations should actively seek input from communities that may be affected by AI systems. This can help identify potential risks and ethical concerns early in the development process, leading to more responsible AI practices.
- "Public Consultations": Hosting public consultations to gather input from affected communities can help organizations understand the potential impacts of their AI systems and address concerns proactively.

3.3 Continuous Monitoring and Evaluation

Implementing processes for continuous monitoring and evaluation of AI systems is essential for identifying and addressing biases, security vulnerabilities, and ethical concerns.

- "Regular Audits": Organizations should conduct regular audits of their AI systems to assess their performance and identify any biases or ethical issues. This can help ensure that AI technologies are functioning as intended and that any issues are promptly addressed.
- "Feedback Mechanisms": Establishing feedback mechanisms that allow users to report concerns or issues with AI systems can help organizations identify and address problems in real-time.

4. The Collaborative Future of Humans and AI

4.1 Human-AI Collaboration

The future of AI will likely involve a collaborative relationship between humans and AI systems, where both can complement each other's strengths.

4.1.1 Augmented Intelligence

Rather than replacing humans, AI can augment human intelligence by providing tools and insights that enhance decision-making and creativity.

- "Human-Centric AI Design": Designing AI systems with a focus on human needs and capabilities can lead to more effective collaboration. This includes creating user-friendly interfaces and ensuring that AI systems are interpretable and explainable.

- "Empowering Workers": AI can empower workers by providing them with data-driven insights and automating routine tasks, allowing them to focus on strategic and creative aspects of their work.

4.1.2 Ethical AI Development

Ensuring that AI technologies are developed ethically is essential for fostering trust and collaboration between humans and AI.

- "Inclusive Development Teams": Building diverse teams of developers and stakeholders can help identify and address potential biases in AI systems. Engaging with various stakeholders can provide valuable insights into the ethical implications of AI technologies.
- "Stakeholder Engagement": Engaging with external stakeholders, including policymakers, ethicists, and community organizations, can help organizations navigate the complexities of AI deployment responsibly.

4.2 Education and Training for the Future

Preparing the workforce for a future where AI plays a significant role requires a focus on education and training.

4.2.1 Curriculum Innovation

Educational institutions should adapt their curricula to include AI literacy, ethics, and interdisciplinary studies that combine technology with social sciences.

- "AI Literacy Programs": Introducing AI literacy programs at all educational levels can help individuals understand AI technologies, their applications, and their implications. This knowledge will empower future generations to engage critically with AI.
- "Interdisciplinary Learning": Encouraging interdisciplinary learning can foster a holistic understanding of AI's impact on society. Students should be exposed to the ethical, social, and economic dimensions of AI alongside technical skills.

4.2.2 Lifelong Learning Initiatives

As the job market evolves, promoting a culture of lifelong learning will be essential for individuals to adapt to changing demands.

- "Access to Continuous Education": Organizations and governments should provide access to continuous education and training programs that enable workers to acquire new skills and stay relevant in an AI-driven economy.
- "Mentorship and Support": Establishing mentorship programs can help individuals navigate their career paths and develop the skills needed to thrive in a rapidly changing job landscape.

5. The Role of Government in AI Governance

5.1 Establishing Regulatory Frameworks

Governments play a crucial role in establishing regulatory frameworks that govern the use of AI technologies.

5.1.1 Comprehensive AI Policies

Developing comprehensive AI policies that address ethical considerations, data protection, and accountability is essential for responsible AI use.

- "Ethical Guidelines": Policymakers should establish ethical guidelines for AI development and deployment that prioritize fairness, accountability, and transparency.
- "Data Protection Regulations": Implementing robust data protection regulations is essential to safeguard individuals' privacy rights in the age of AI.

5.1.2 Accountability and Liability Frameworks

Establishing accountability and liability frameworks for AI systems is crucial for addressing ethical dilemmas and ensuring responsible AI use. Policymakers should clarify who is responsible for the outcomes of AI decision-making and establish mechanisms for addressing negative impacts.

- "Liability for AI Decisions": Policymakers should define liability for AI decisions, determining whether it rests with developers, organizations, or the AI systems themselves. This clarity can help ensure accountability and encourage responsible practices.
- "Reporting Mechanisms": Implementing reporting mechanisms for AI-related incidents can help organizations identify and address issues promptly. This includes establishing channels for individuals to report concerns about AI systems.

5.2 Supporting Research and Innovation

Governments should invest in research and innovation to advance the responsible development of AI technologies. This includes funding research on ethical AI, bias mitigation, and the societal impacts of AI, as well as supporting initiatives that promote collaboration between academia, industry, and government.

5.2.1 Funding Ethical AI Research

Allocating funding for research on ethical AI practices can help organizations develop fair and unbiased systems. Policymakers should prioritize research initiatives that focus on bias mitigation, transparency, and accountability in AI technologies.

- "Grants for Ethical AI Projects": Providing grants for projects that explore ethical AI development can encourage innovation and promote responsible practices in the field.
- "Collaborative Research Initiatives": Supporting collaborative research initiatives between academia and industry can foster knowledge sharing and drive advancements in ethical AI practices.

5.2.2 Promoting Public-Private Partnerships

Encouraging public-private partnerships can facilitate collaboration between government agencies and private organizations in the development of responsible AI technologies. These partnerships can leverage resources and expertise to address common challenges.

- "Joint Research Programs": Establishing joint research programs can enable organizations to work together on ethical AI initiatives, sharing best practices and resources to drive innovation.
- "Innovation Hubs": Creating innovation hubs that bring together government, industry, and academia can foster collaboration and support the development of responsible AI technologies.

5.3 Encouraging International Cooperation

AI is a global phenomenon, and addressing its risks requires international cooperation. Policymakers should work together to establish global standards and best practices for AI development and deployment, ensuring that ethical considerations are prioritized across borders.

5.3.1 Global AI Governance Frameworks

Developing global AI governance frameworks can help establish common standards for ethical AI practices. Policymakers should collaborate with international organizations to create guidelines that promote responsible AI use worldwide.

- "International Agreements": Establishing international agreements on AI ethics and governance can facilitate cooperation among countries and promote the responsible development of AI technologies.
- "Cross-Border Data Regulations": Policymakers should work towards harmonizing data protection regulations across borders to ensure that individuals' privacy rights are upheld globally.

5.3.2 Sharing Best Practices

Encouraging the sharing of best practices among countries can help promote responsible AI development. Policymakers should facilitate platforms for knowledge exchange and collaboration on ethical AI initiatives.

- "Global Conferences and Workshops": Hosting global conferences and workshops on AI ethics can provide opportunities for stakeholders to share insights and experiences, fostering a collaborative approach to addressing AI risks.
- "Collaborative Research Networks": Establishing collaborative research networks can facilitate knowledge sharing and drive advancements in ethical AI practices across countries. These networks can support joint research initiatives and promote the dissemination of best practices.

6. Conclusion

➤ Mitigating the risks of AI is essential for harnessing its benefits while minimizing negative impacts on society. By developing fair and unbiased AI systems, protecting individual privacy, creating jobs that are not easily automated, and fostering a culture of responsible AI use, organizations can navigate the complexities of AI deployment effectively.

➤ Policymakers play a crucial role in this process by establishing regulatory frameworks, supporting research and innovation, and encouraging international cooperation. The collaboration among individuals, organizations, and policymakers will be vital in shaping a future where AI serves as a tool for positive societal impact. As we move forward, it is imperative to prioritize ethical considerations and implement practices that ensure AI technologies contribute to the greater good, fostering a future where technology enhances human potential and well-being.

➤ The journey towards a responsible AI ecosystem is ongoing and requires the collective efforts of individuals, organizations, and governments. By fostering a culture of responsibility, leveraging technology for ethical AI, and engaging the global community, we can navigate the complexities of AI technologies effectively.

➢ As we move forward, it is essential to prioritize ethical considerations and implement practices that ensure AI technologies contribute positively to society. The path ahead will require continuous dialogue, collaboration, and innovation to create an environment where AI serves as a force for good, enhancing human potential and addressing the challenges we face as a global community. By committing to responsible AI development and deployment, we can build a future where technology empowers individuals, fosters inclusivity, and drives sustainable progress for all.

www.ingramcontent.com/pod-product-compliance
Lightning Source LLC
LaVergne TN
LVHW051330050326
832903LV00031B/3454

9 798316 242870